The *Story of*

BASKETBALL

REVISED EDITION

Dave Anderson

Foreword by **Grant Hill**

For Ellis
KEEP READING
AND KEEP STUDYING

Dave Anderson

A BEECH TREE PAPERBACK BOOK

New York

Permission for photographs is gratefully acknowledged: page
3—AP/Wide World Photos; pages 10, 28, 42, 51, 54, 55, 59,
63, 74, 82, 86, 89, 91, 97, 99, 100, 102, 110, 128—UPI/
Corbis-Bettmann; pages 11, 14, 17, 18, 21, 23, 137—Naismith
Memorial Basketball Hall of Fame (Wayne Patterson, research
specialist); pages 15, 19, 20, 25, 35, 39, 45, 48, 53, 61, 71, 93,
105, 113, 120, 126, 133—UPI/Bettmann Newsphotos; page
27—Harlem Globetrotters; page 31—Stanford Media Relations;
page 56—University of California, Los Angeles; pages 67, 69,
95, 129—Reuters/Corbis-Bettmann; pages 77, 108, 131—
Reuters/Bettmann; page 78—Jed Jacobsohn/ALLSPORT; page
124—Jim Cund/ALLSPORT; page 125—AP Photo/Scott
Troyanos; page 132—Scott Ball/ University of California; page
134—University of North Carolina; page 139—Al Bello/
ALLSPORT; page 140—Jonathan Daniel/ALLSPORT

Published by William Morrow and Company, Inc.
1350 Avenue of the Americas, New York, NY 10019

Printed in the United States of America.

The Library of Congress has cataloged the Morrow Junior
Books edition of *The Story of Basketball* as follows:
Anderson, Dave.
The story of basketball/Dave Anderson.
p. cm.
Includes index.
Summary: Presents an overview of the history of basketball
from its beginning in 1891 and profiles some notable players
and coaches of modern times.
ISBN 0-688-14316-4
1. Basketball—Juvenile literature. 2. Basketball—History—
Juvenile literature. [1. Basketball—History. 2. Basketball
players.] I. Title. GV885.A458 1988 796.32'32—DC20
96-46147 CIP AC

10 9 8 7 6 5 4 3 2
First revised Beech Tree edition, 1997.
ISBN 0-688-14317-2

*I*AM THE FIRST TO ADMIT I'VE BEEN LUCKY IN MY BASKETBALL career. While at Duke University, I played on two national championship teams, and I was on the 1996 Olympic team that won a gold medal in Atlanta. Now I'm trying to help the Detroit Pistons win a National Basketball Association title.

But life is more than basketball. When I was growing up, my parents, Janet and Calvin Hill, always stressed to me the importance of education, athletics, and the right people.

In its own way, this book, *The Story of Basketball*, emphasizes the importance of all three: education, in detailing the history of what has been truly America's game for more than a century; athletics, in that basketball is probably the most athletic game of all; and the right people, in the sense of its greatest players and coaches.

Any perspective on the best teams, players, and coaches of today, in both the NBA and college basketball, is framed by the knowledge of the best teams, players, and coaches of yesterday. I would begin with the Original

Celtics, who dominated the game more than half a century ago with fundamentals that are still so important.

A vital part of this book is its insight into what basketball represents: the blending of five players with one ball to create a team. For all the points I've scored, for all the games in which I was on the winning team, I was only one of five players on the floor. If it weren't for the contributions of the other four players and the coach, none of us would have been on that winning team.

Like most NBA players, I'm known for my physical skills—being able to soar to the basket for a slam dunk or to swat an opponent's shot out of the air. But basketball is also a game of mental skills—knowing when to shoot, when to pass, how to stay a step ahead of your opponent on defense, how to time your leap for a rebound, when to listen to the advice of your coach and your more experienced teammates.

As I wrote in my own book, *Change the Game* (Warner Books), my Duke coach, Mike Krzyzewski, always challenged me by saying, "Don't be afraid to be great." And as I like to tell youngsters now, "Don't be afraid to do the right thing," on and off the court.

That sense of the game—and much more—is here in *The Story of Basketball*, a book for everyone who ever enjoyed this wonderful sport, invented in 1896 in a little YMCA gym in Springfield, Massachusetts, and now played and watched by people all over the world.

Contents

*part*One

IN THE BEGINNING

Dr. Naismith's Peach Baskets

FOR SOME YOUNGSTERS, IT STARTS WITH AIMING A ROLLED-UP wad of paper at a wastebasket. Others toss an empty soda can into a trash bin or flip an apple core into a garbage bag. But for Larry Bird, the legendary Boston Celtic forward from French Lick, Indiana, it started with a coffee can.

"When we were growing up," Bird says of himself and his brothers, "before we got a real basketball hoop, we used a coffee can and tried to shoot one of those small sponge-rubber balls through it."

Basketball is big business now, performed on big stages in big arenas by big players for big money. The National Basketball Association playoffs and the college Final Four are seen on television by millions. High school tournaments stir entire states. But it's also a game for kids in gyms and playgrounds and rural backyards, shooting a basketball at a hoop, sometimes with others, sometimes alone. For nearly a century, from the Original Celtics to the Boston Celtics, from the two-handed set shot to the slam dunk, a ball and a hoop have endured as the essence of the sport, not that much different from the leather soccer ball that Dr. James Naismith tossed to his students late in 1891 and the wooden peach baskets nailed to the balcony railings at each end of the gymnasium in Springfield, Massachusetts.

Unlike other sports, basketball is considered to be a pure American sport, invented in America for Americans. Baseball evolved from rounders, a British game. Football evolved from soccer and rugby, other British games. Golf is believed to have been developed by Scottish shepherds, tennis by French clerics, hockey by Canadian soldiers. Horse racing, track-and-field, swimming, and boxing are as old as humankind. But the beginning of basketball has been documented by its inventor.

Then thirty years old, with a bushy mustache, Canadian-born Naismith was a physical education instructor at the International Young Men's Christian Association Training School, now Springfield College. In that era, the school trained physical education instructors for YMCAs throughout the nation.

Dr. James Naismith, the father of basketball

In addition to the daily classroom work, an hour of physical education activity was required. In the fall the students played what was then a new game, football. In the spring they went outdoors to play baseball. But during the winter months they were confined indoors for calisthenics and marching. When the students complained, gymnastics were substituted. But the students continued to complain. Naismith, who had spent three years studying for the ministry before deciding to devote himself to physical education, was asked to take over the class by Dr. Luther S. Gulick, the head of the school's physical education department.

"In the fall of '91," Naismith wrote in 1937 while a professor at the University of Kansas, the physical fitness directors of the country "had come to the conclusion that maybe neither the German, Swedish, or French system gave us the kind of work that would hold our membership in the Y's.

"We decided that there should be a game that could be played indoors in the evening and during the winter seasons. I began to think of the fundamental principles of all games. I discovered that in all team games some kind of a ball was used. The next step was to appreciate the fact that football was rough because you had to allow the defense to tackle because the offense ran with the ball. Accordingly, if the offense didn't have an opportunity to run with the

In this YMCA building, the first game was played in 1891.

ball, there would be no necessity for tackling, and we would thus eliminate roughness.

"This is the fundamental principle of basketball.

"The next step was to secure some kind of a goal through which the ball could be passed. In thinking of upright goals, the fact was brought out that the more force that was put on the ball, the more likelihood there was of having it pass through the goal. It then occurred to me that if the ball were thrown in a curve, it would not be necessary or advisable to put too much force on the ball.

"I decided that by making the goal horizontal the ball would have to be thrown in a curve, minimizing the severe driving of a ball. In order to avoid having the defense congregate around the goal, it was placed above their heads, so that once the ball left the individual's hands, it was not likely to be interfered with.

"Then rules were made to eliminate roughness such as shoulder-ing, pushing, kicking, etc. The ball was to be handled with the hands only. It could not be drawn into the body and thus encourage rough-ness.

"The manner of putting the ball into play was then considered. Two individuals were selected and took their stations in the middle of the floor. The ball was thrown up so as to land between them, giving as nearly equal chance as possible. The nearest approach to the ball needed was the soccer ball, which we selected.

"To get goals, we used a couple of old peach baskets, hanging one at each end of the gym. From this, basketball developed."

The Original Rules

Before the first basketball game was played in the Springfield gym, Dr. Naismith posted a copy of his original thirteen rules, some of which have never had to be changed:

1. The ball may be thrown in any direction with one or both hands.
2. The ball may be batted in any direction with one or both hands (never with the fist).
3. A player cannot run with the ball. The player must throw it from the spot on which he catches it, allowance to be made for a man who catches the ball when running if he tries to stop.
4. The ball must be held in the hands; the arms or body must not be used for holding it.
5. No shouldering, holding, pushing, tripping, or striking in any way the person of an opponent shall be allowed; the first infringement of this rule by any player shall count as a foul, the second shall disqualify him until the next goal is made, or, if there was evident intent to injure the person, for the whole of the game; no substitute shall be allowed.
6. A foul is striking at the ball with the fist, violation of Rules 3, 4, and such as described in Rule 5.
7. If either side makes three consecutive fouls, it shall count

as a goal for the opponents. (Consecutive means without the opponents in the meantime making a foul.)

8. A goal shall be made when the ball is thrown or batted from the ground into the basket and stays there, provided those defending the goal do not touch or disturb the goal. If the ball rests on the edges, and the opponent moves the basket, it shall count as a goal.

9. When the ball goes out of bounds, it shall be thrown into the field and played by the person first touching it. He has a right to hold it unmolested for five seconds. In case of a dispute, the umpire shall throw it straight into the field. The thrower-in is allowed five seconds. If he holds it longer, it shall go to the opponent. If any side persists in delaying the game, the umpire shall call a foul on that side.

10. The umpire shall be judge of the men and shall note the fouls and notify the referee when three consecutive fouls have been made. He shall have power to disqualify men according to Rule 5.

11. The referee shall be judge of the ball and shall decide when the ball is in play, in bounds, to which side it belongs, and shall keep the time. He shall decide when a goal has been made, and keep account of the goals, with any other duties that are usually performed by a referee.

12. The time shall be two fifteen-minute halves, with five minutes' rest between halves.

13. The side making the most goals in that time shall be declared the winner. In case of a draw, the game may, by agreement of the captains, be continued until another goal is made.

Quirks of fate determined the shape and height of the goals. Naismith had planned for players to shoot at a box, but when none

The YMCA gym, before the peach baskets were nailed up

was available, he had the janitor nail the peach baskets to the balcony railing, which happened to be ten feet above the floor. Just as ninety feet between bases has proved to be the proper distance in baseball, a hoop ten feet above the floor has proved to be the proper height in basketball.

Naismith also planned that any number of players could participate in a basketball game. In the very first game, all eighteen members of his physical education class were on the court, nine to a side. But by the turn of the century, a team was reduced to no more than five players on the court at any one time. By then, a field goal had been established as being worth 2 points, a successful foul shot as 1 point. The original rule regarding an automatic goal for the team that had been fouled three consecutive times was soon replaced by free throws.

Other elements needed time to be refined, notably the center jump after each basket. When the center jump rule was repealed in 1937, it opened up the game, enabling teams to employ the fast break and creating higher scores that were more appealing to the public.

In the early years, 20 points often was enough to win—not 20 points for one player, but for an entire team. And until 1923, one player was allowed to shoot all of his team's foul shots. Around that time, backboards were standardized. Before that, wood was optional. Some backboards were made of wire, and occasionally the hoop simply was hung on a tall pole without a backboard. The court often was surrounded by a wire cage, inspiring the term "cagers" as a synonym for the players.

Following the introduction of Naismith's rules, one of the instructor's students suggested that the game be called Naismithball. But the inventor baptized it basketball.

Shortly after the YMCA students returned early in 1892 from their Christmas vacation, Naismith organized the first team. It had nine players. The first game between two different organizations occurred in Springfield that February, with YMCA teams from the Central and Armory Hill branches in Springfield playing to a 2–2 tie. In a rematch a month later, Armory Hill won 1–0. Around that same time, the first women's basketball game involved a team of Springfield girls against a group of women teachers. One of the players in that game, Maude Sherman, so impressed Naismith that he married her. Two women's colleges, Vassar and Smith, each added basketball to its athletic program

The first team, with Dr. Naismith in middle row (right)

later that year, while Vanderbilt had the first men's college team, in March 1893. Four years later, Yale defeated the University of Pennsylvania, 32–10, in what is considered the first college game with five-player teams. By then several YMCA leagues had been formed. When the first "Championship of America" tournament was staged in Brooklyn, New York, in April 1896, East District defeated Brooklyn Central, 4–0.

But many YMCA leaders considered basketball to be too rough and too disruptive of the normal physical education program. "The game," a YMCA publication complained in an 1894 editorial, "could never and should never be allowed to take the place of all other exercise in the gymnasium." As a result, some YMCA players turned to armories, skating rinks, dance halls, and even barns as game sites. In order to rent the court, they charged admission. That's how pro basketball was born in a game in Trenton, New Jersey, in 1896.

Each player was paid fifteen dollars apiece, with the Trenton captain, Fred Cooper, receiving a one-dollar bonus. The pros dressed the part. They wore velvet trunks, long tights, and frilled stockings. One of their players, Dutch Wohlfarth, even dribbled without watching the lopsided ball.

The First Pro League

In 1898 the first pro league, the National Basketball League, was formed with six teams from the Philadelphia area—Trenton, Camden, Millville, the Pennsylvania Bicycle Club, the Hancock Athletic Club, and the Germantown Club. Trenton won two championships; then the league disbanded.

The first pros to command significant money were the Buffalo Germans, organized in 1895 as an unpaid YMCA team of fourteen-year-old boys. Over two decades, they had a 792-86 record, including a 111-game winning streak. Their reputation eventually earned guarantees of as much as five hundred dollars, then a huge sum, for a three-game series. Other leagues also had been created—notably the Central League, which existed from 1906 to 1912, and the Eastern League, from 1909 to 1923. But from one night to another, the players often switched leagues and teams in order to make more money. Barney Sedran, a 5-4 guard who scored 17 baskets in a game shooting at a hoop without a backboard, led his Carbondale, Pennsylvania, team to 35 consecutive victories in the Tri-County League, but that same season he also played a complete schedule with the Utica team of the New York State League. Perhaps because of his size, Sedran was among those who favored the adoption of rope netting that replaced the wire cages.

"Players would be thrown against the wire," Sedran once said, "and most of us would get cut."

Another problem for the players was the floor itself, especially in the dance halls, where the floor was waxed to cater to dancers, not to the basketball players who slipped on it. Most of the courts were small, no more than sixty feet by forty feet. To support the roof or a floor above, some courts had a pillar, or post, in the middle. When an offensive player ran his defender into that post, he used what was called the "post" play, a term that still applies today in referring to how a center such as Shaquille O'Neal sets up in a high "post" or a low "post," in order to use himself as a screen for a teammate.

In college basketball, Yale's team toured in 1900, then organized an Eastern League in 1901 with Harvard, Columbia, Cornell, and Princeton. Also that year Holy Cross, Dartmouth, Williams, Amherst, and Trinity organized the New England League. By 1908 little Wabash (Indiana) College, with a 66-3 record over four seasons, claimed to be the nation's best team.

But the best players were the pros, even though

Barney Sedran, a small wonder at 5-4 and 118 pounds

At 6-6, Ed Wachter was the first of the tall centers.

they were not earning much money. Two of the most celebrated teams were Basloe's Oswego (New York) Indians, who had a 121-6 record during the 1914–15 season after winning three out of four from the Buffalo Germans the previous season, and the Troy (New York) Trojans with Ed Wachter, a 6-6 center who later was the Harvard coach. On a 1915 barnstorming tour of the West, the Trojans won all 35 games while popularizing the bounce pass and what was then considered a fast break, racing to the basket after the center jump. (All technical terms are defined in the glossary at the back of the book.)

Around that same time, a teenage stringbean, Joe Lapchick, was earning five dollars a game with the Yonkers Bantams. Within a few years he would develop into basketball's most feared center on its most feared team.

Original Celtics and Globetrotters

SHORTLY AFTER WORLD WAR I, THE ORIGINAL CELTICS revolutionized basketball, on and off the court. For nearly a decade, the Celtics, most of whom had grown up in New York City's tough West Side neighborhood, were a traveling team that played everywhere and anywhere. But for the 1922–23 season their promoter, Jim Furey, hired a Manhattan armory for Sunday night games and signed his six players to exclusive contracts with guaranteed salaries. On that team were Pete Barry, Dutch Dehnert, Horace "Horse" Haggerty, Johnny Beckman, Joe Trippe, and Ernie Reich; the coach was Johnny Witty, who played when needed. In the natural turnover of the roster, Furey later signed Nat Holman, Joe Lapchick, Davey Banks, Chris Leonard, Carl Husta, and Nat Hickey.

When the Celtics weren't playing in New York, they barnstormed, playing local teams in various cities. One night in

Nat Holman, backcourt leader of the Original Celtics

Chattanooga, Tennessee, they were playing the Railities, a local industrial team. Holman had to return to New York for business reasons, and the Celtics hired Benny Borgmann as his replacement for the one-night stand.

"The Railities were using a standing guard, something which has long since gone out of basketball," Dehnert once recalled. "He stood right on his own foul line and never went upcourt, even when his own team had the ball. During a time-out, Beckman said, 'We'll have to move that guard out of there—he's breaking up our passes when we cut.' I volunteered to stand in front of the guard, explaining that instead of him breaking up our passes, they could pass to me and I could give it back."

When a "great light dawned," Dutch Dehnert reacted in the pivot.

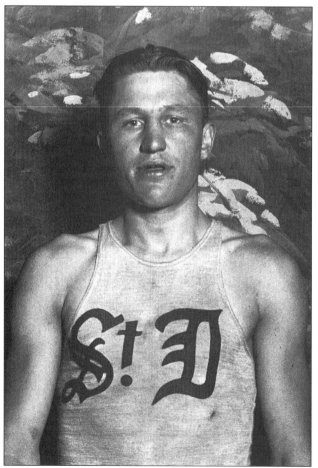

When the game resumed, Dehnert stood in front of the Chattanooga guard, took a pass from Beckman, then passed to Borgmann, who passed to Barry.

"And then," Dehnert said, "Barry passed to me, kept coming, and I passed right back to him. All of a sudden, a great light dawned and I took time out. We all went into a huddle and discussed the possibilities of the maneuver we had accidentally hit on. This was the pivot play, but we didn't even know it at the time. A couple of minutes later, the standing guard, in an effort to bat the ball out of my hands, moved around to my right side. All I had to do was pivot to my left, take one step, and lay the ball up for a basket."

The pivot play, so common now, suddenly was the talk of basketball, an attraction in itself.

"See the Original Pivot Play," blared posters for Celtic games, "Starring the One and Only Dutch Dehnert."

The Celtics also pulled the first "switch" on defense, their players switching to the closest offensive player rather than covering the same player, as other teams did. At first this tactic confused Lapchick, a slim 6-5 center who later would teach the maneuver as the coach of St. John's University and the New York Knicks.

"Your defensive duties entailed more than merely guarding the fellow who jumped against you," Lapchick once explained. "They were constantly switching on defense, and I couldn't figure out how they did it, except by instinct. I was always getting in somebody's way. My teammates were getting picked off right and left. Johnny Witty saved me."

Later a coach, Joe Lapchick learned to play without the ball.

Lapchick's teammates were impatient, but Witty, the Celtics' coach, took him aside for a pep talk.

"He told me," Lapchick recalled, "what a great basketball player I was going to be, with my height and my speed, as soon as I mastered the technique of switching. 'It isn't how many goals you get, Joe,' Witty used to say, 'or how often you get the tap. We know what you can do with the ball. It's how good you are without the ball that determines how good a basketball player you are.' And there, I think, Witty summed up the creed of the Celtics—it's how good you are without the ball that makes you a basketball player."

Lapchick was referring to the Original Celtics, but he might have been referring to today's Boston Celtics, or to any of today's best NBA teams or college teams. Players on those teams know how to play *without* the ball, not merely with the ball.

The Original Celtics were so good, the American Basketball League couldn't live with them or without them. Inspired in 1925 by George Preston Marshall, the Washington, D.C., laundryman who later owned the pro football Redskins, the ABL had franchises in Washington, Boston, Brooklyn, Rochester, Fort Wayne, Chicago, Cleveland, Buffalo, and Detroit. But without the Celtics, the ABL had no credibility, especially when the Celtics were thrashing ABL teams on their barnstorming tours. After one season of embarrassment, ABL teams refused to play the Celtics, who then reluctantly joined the ABL in 1926 in order to stay solvent. When the Celtics won the next two ABL championships, the team was broken up, its talent spread among other teams for competitive balance. But without the Celtics as its flagship franchise, the ABL folded in 1931.

The Ballroom Rens

Although the Celtics were reunited briefly, the Depression diluted their barnstorming income. Even in New York, they had been somewhat upstaged by the Rens, an all-black team that played at the Renaissance Casino Ballroom in Harlem. The Rens often shared the ballroom with Count Basie's band.

During the 1926–27 season, the Rens had established their credibility by splitting a six-game series against the Celtics, with a top ticket at one dollar a game, twenty-five cents more than the usual price. Founded in 1922 by Bob Douglas, a West Indian native, the Rens often were the victims of racial prejudice on their barnstorming tours. In that era, some hotels and restaurants wouldn't accept blacks. The players often had to sleep and eat in their bus. James "Pappy" Ricks, Clarence "Fat" Jenkins, and Eyre "Bruiser" Saitch were among the original Rens players. They were joined later by Charles "Tarzan" Cooper, Wee Willie Smith, Bill Yancey, and John "Casey" Holt to form the seven-man squad that had a 473-49 record, including an 88-game winning streak, from 1932 to 1936.

"Tarzan Cooper," Joe Lapchick said, "was the best center I ever played against."

The Rens: Clarence Jenkins, Bill Yancey, John Holt, James Ricks, Eyre Saitch, Charles Cooper, and Wee Willie Smith. Inset: Owner Robert L. Douglas, who organized the club in 1922

   In 1939 the Rens, who had a 112-7 record that season, won the world pro tournament in Chicago, defeating the Oshkosh (Wisconsin) All-Stars in the final after having eliminated the Harlem Globetrotters earlier. The next year the Globetrotters won the pro title, defeating the Rens in the semifinal and the Chicago Bruins in the final, 31–29, in overtime. At the time the Trotters were mostly a serious basketball team, unlike today's show team, which plays strictly for laughs. Their roly-poly founder, Abe Saperstein, was born in London but grew up in Chicago, where he was a 5-3 basketball player. After two years at the University of Illinois, he began coaching a hotel team, the Savoy Big Five, which played between dances in the ballroom that inspired the "Stompin' at the Savoy" tune of that era. When the hotel decided that the all-black team wasn't attracting enough dancers, Saperstein renamed it.

"We chose Harlem," he once said, "because Harlem was to our black players what Jerusalem is to me. As for Globetrotters, well, we had dreams. We hoped to travel."

Through the years, the Globetrotters have performed before nearly one hundred million people in nearly one hundred countries. Introduced to the whistling beat of "Sweet Georgia Brown," the classic Brother Bones recording, they gather at midcourt in their star-spangled red, white, blue, and gold uniforms and flip the ball behind their backs, off their heads, between their legs, along an outstretched arm, over their shoulders, and, as if it were a top, spin it on their index fingers. Ironically the Globetrotters did not appear in Harlem, a predominantly black area of upper Manhattan in New York City, until 1968, when they conducted a schoolyard clinic there. By that time, however, they had actually trotted all over the globe.

Khrushchev's Greeting

During their first trip to Moscow in 1959, the Globetrotters were strolling near the Kremlin when a limousine suddenly stopped. Nikita Khrushchev stepped out and waved to the players. "Ah, basketball," the Soviet Premier said.

On that trip the Soviets paid Saperstein in fur pelts and postage stamps instead of cash. In India he once had to take carpets and cloth. But the Trotters' most historic appearance developed in 1951, when Saperstein was asked by American officials in postwar Germany to counteract the World Communist Youth rallies there. Accompanying the Globies on that tour was Jesse Owens, the black American athlete whom Adolf Hitler declined to shake hands with after Owens had won four track-and-field gold medals at the Berlin Olympics in 1936. When the Trotters appeared in the Olympic Stadium, more than seventy-five thousand people assembled to enjoy the game and to cheer Owens, whose dramatic entrance occurred at halftime when he stepped out of a helicopter.

"That presentation in Berlin," Saperstein once said, "proved to be the highlight of my entire career."

On their European tours, the Globies have performed for the Pope on six occasions. Over the years the Trotters have played basketball in bullrings, on tennis courts, and even inside the French Foreign Legion command post at Sedi, Bel Abbes, Algeria, on the edge of the Sahara Desert.

On their later American tours, the Globetrotters traveled in two custom-built buses with the seats spaced to enable the long-legged players to stretch out and snooze. But when the Globetrotters traveled to their first game outside Chicago, on January 7, 1927, they stuffed themselves into Saperstein's Model T Ford for the trip to Hinckley, Illinois,

Abe Saperstein "had dreams," and his Globetrotters toured the world.

about fifty miles away. Their seventy-five-dollar fee was split seven ways—one share to each of the five players, two to Saperstein as coach and promoter. But soon the Trotters were traveling in two secondhand cars.

"The good one was the club car, the other one was the baggage car," Saperstein once joked. "The club car had only seventy-nine thousand miles on it when we got it."

In small towns, those Trotters often appeared on makeshift courts. One in Des Plaines, Illinois, had six pillars, inspiring the players to break free for a shot by running their defenders into the pillars. One in Harlem, Montana, was a drained swimming pool that was downhill (or uphill) at one end. And in Shelby, Montana, three cowboys with pistols in their belts suggested that the local team had not lost in three years, and it might be safer for the Trotters to lose.

"After we beat them pretty easily," Saperstein once recalled, "we realized why they needed outside help to compile a record like that."

The Trotters simply were too good for those small-town teams. In

Woodfire, British Columbia, they once routed the local lumberjacks, 112–20. Against some farmers in Atlantic, Iowa, one of the early Globetrotters, Al "Punt" Rollins, scored 75 points, still believed to be the team's one-player scoring record for one game. Saperstein remembered a Montana blizzard when he, seven players, and four strangers from another snowbound car huddled in a prairie shack where a rancher and nine sheep had found shelter.

"When people ask me what it's like to take a basketball team on tour," Saperstein said, "I ask them if they've ever inhaled for three days in a twenty-by-fourteen room with thirteen people and nine sheep."

For more than two decades, the Globetrotters indeed were a basketball team, not a show. But as they toured night after night, they learned to take a breather by inserting some fancy ball-handling into the games.

"You make the ball do the work, not yourself," Inman Jackson, their center in those early years, once explained. "You create an illusion of action while you're resting."

That illusion dazzled the spectators in the high school and dance halls where the Trotters usually appeared. Jackson would roll the ball up one arm, across the back of his shoulders, and down the other arm. Louis "Babe" Pressley would throw the ball across the court with so much backspin it would bounce back to him as though on a string. But they were a skilled team with skilled players, as they proved by winning the 1940 world professional tournament for independent touring teams as well as National Basketball League (NBL) teams.

The NBL had been formed in 1937 with franchises in several Midwestern cities, including Akron, Ohio; Fort Wayne, Indiana; and Oshkosh, Wisconsin. Franchises were at various times awarded to Chicago, Detroit, Cleveland, Minneapolis, Rochester, and Syracuse, among others. Among its best players were John Wooden, later the UCLA coach, and Bill "Red" Holzman, later the New York Knicks' coach, as well as George Mikan, the 6-11 center who later would lead the Minneapolis Lakers to three NBA titles.

In 1948 the Globetrotters stunned the Lakers—who, led by Mikan, had just won the NBL championship—61–59, then split the other games in their series. Two years later the Trotters won 13 of 18 games against a touring College All-Star team featuring Bob Cousy, later a ten-time All-NBA guard for the Boston Celtics.

Goose Tatum's "Reems"

While more than holding their own against the Lakers and the College All-Stars, those Globetrotters also were the most entertaining team in basketball history.

Marques Haynes, a magical dribbler, weaved in and out of defenders, bounced the ball between their legs, dropped to one knee and sometimes to both knees. Nat "Sweetwater" Clifton, a husky 6-8 forward, later joined the New York Knicks. Babe Pressley, the long-armed captain, was the other for-

Marques Haynes, the magical dribbler

ward, Ermer Robinson the other guard. But the primary box-office attraction was Reece "Goose" Tatum, the high-stepping center whose outstretched arms created an eighty-four-inch wingspan, a natural scorer who once produced 30 points against the College All-Stars. More importantly, Tatum was also a natural clown.

Tatum created many of the "reems," the comic routines that made the Globetrotters famous. He spun the ball on one fingertip. He let the ball roll down one of

his long arms, then flicked a finger to stop it. He stuffed the ball under his jersey, then pretended he didn't know where it was. During a time-out, he tiptoed over to the other team's huddle, leaned in to hear what was being talked about, then hurried back to his teammates.

One of Tatum's favorites was to fall to the floor while taking a shot, pretending he had been knocked unconscious. While the spectators gasped, his teammates huddled around him and the public-address announcer would ask, "Is there a doctor in the house?" Then one of his Globetrotter teammates would remove one of Tatum's size-fourteen sneakers from his foot and hold it under Tatum's nose. With a sudden leap, Goose would jump up, his eyes and mouth twitching, then strut around the court while his teammates gaped. He was to basketball clowning what Emmett Kelly was to circus clowning.

"Goose was a genius," a Globetrotter teammate, Leon Hilliard, once said. "He had a feeling for his audience, for the situation, that was unbelievable. He could be so funny, we'd all be laughing right out there on the court."

But a Globetrotter "reem" sometimes required the opposing team to stand still when Goose Tatum and his successors in later years, Meadowlark Lemon and Goose Ausbie, put on a show. Eventually, as the NBA signed the best black players, the Globetrotters emerged as entertainers rather than competitors. They traveled with a team known as the Washington Generals, who often resembled five stooges.

"We won't hurt the Globies' show," Herman "Red" Klotz, the Generals' coach and owner, once said. "When they start doing a reem, we don't mess 'em up. The quicker they get it over with, the quicker we get the ball. But if they make a mistake, if they lose the ball, I've always told my players to grab it and go."

Although the Globetrotters' winning streak of 8,829 games ended on September 12, 1995, in a 91–85 loss to Kareem Abdul-Jabbar's All-Stars in Vienna, Austria, nobody took the streak seriously. This was a team to enjoy, not to root for. And certainly not to root against. In

Nobody enjoyed basketball more than Goose Tatum.

their football reem, a player drop-kicks the ball into the basket, a trick Goose Tatum did nearly half a century ago. In their water-gag reem, a player appears to toss a bucket of water at the audience, but the bucket is really filled with shredded paper.

"We've got dozens of reems," Curly Neal, a Trotter for nearly two decades, once said, "but the others don't mean much."

With the retirement of Sweet Lou Dunbar in 1995, Paul "Showtime" Gaffney moved to center stage for the reems, but in the evolution of basketball, the Globetrotters, for all their antics, provided basketball with a new dimension—individual creativity. One of the Original Celtics, Dutch Dehnert, appreciated that.

"You have to give the nod to the Trotters for their speed and their fancy stuff," Dehnert said more than thirty years ago. "We had two basic plays, the pivot and the give-and-go. But the Trotters can feint you out of the building a dozen different ways."

For the Original Celtics and the early Globetrotters, their arenas were small. So were many of the players. But basketball was about to be played in America's biggest arenas, by some of its biggest men.

Hank Luisetti and George Mikan

FOR NEARLY HALF A CENTURY, EASTERN TEAMS HAD DOMINATED basketball. They knew how to control the ball, how to play man-to-man defense. What they didn't know was that in a San Francisco playground, Angelo "Hank" Luisetti was about to change the way Eastern players and everybody else shot the ball. And the change happened by accident, as most changes do. When he began shooting the ball as a boy, Hank wasn't strong enough to reach the basket the way everybody else did, two-handed.

Stanford's Hank Luisetti, the first one-hand shooter

"I started throwing the ball with one hand," he says. "It happened to go in."

As long as Hank Luisetti played basketball, it continued to go in. Wisely his coaches never tried to force him to shoot with two hands—especially his Stanford University coach, John Bunn, who was a disciple of Dr. James Naismith as a University of Kansas player. When most coaches were ordering their players to remain in one area of the court on offense, Bunn let Luisetti wander.

"I always started at right forward," Luisetti says, "but sometimes I'd find myself playing guard or playing in the post."

As a sophomore during the 1935–36 season, this 6-2 shooter averaged 14.3 points a game. Not much by today's standards, when college teams occasionally score more than 100 points, but a stunning total when teams rarely scored 45 points. In a Pacific Coast Conference championship series against Washington, Luisetti scored 32 points in 32 minutes. With his team trailing Southern Cal by 15 points with 11 minutes remaining, he scored 24 of his 30 points for a 51–47 victory. Even so, the Eastern establishment sneered at Luisetti's statistics. Maybe he could get away with those one-handed shots out West, but when Stanford played Long Island University at Madison Square Garden on December 31, 1936, the dark-haired junior surely would discover that Eastern teams really knew how to play basketball—and how to shoot.

"There's only one way to shoot, and that's with two hands," said Nat Holman, the Original Celtic who was the City College of New York coach. "I'll quit if I have to teach one-handed shots to win."

Although no official champion was determined until 1939, when Oregon won the first National Collegiate Athletic Association tournament, LIU was rated among the nation's best college teams. Coached by Clair Bee, the Blackbirds were on a 43-game winning streak that included a 26-0 record the previous season. Luisetti and his teammates also were expected to be awed by the sellout crowd at the Garden, suddenly the nation's most famous basketball arena.

Ned Irish had taken college basketball out of the musty gyms and put it in the Garden, not far from the bright lights of Broadway and Times Square.

As a young sportswriter with the *New York World-Telegram*, Irish was assigned to cover a basketball game at the Manhattan College gym. Finding the doorway blocked by dozens of people who were unable to buy tickets, Irish crawled in through a back window, ripping his best pair of pants. Irish decided that college basketball deserved a bigger stage. On December 29, 1934, he promoted the Garden's first college doubleheader—New York University against Notre Dame and St. John's against Westminster. It attracted 16,188 spectators, a near sellout. College basketball had arrived. Two years later, Hank Luisetti arrived for his Garden debut, along with 17,623 curious customers. Soon after the game began, Luisetti scored on a one-hander over Art Hillhouse, a 6-6 center.

"You lucky stiff," Hillhouse said.

Not long after that, Luisetti scored on another one-hander, but this time Hillhouse didn't say a word. By halftime Stanford had a 22–14 lead, and as Luisetti and his teammates walked to their dressing room, they were awarded a standing ovation. In the second half Luisetti dominated the 45–31 rout, not only because of his 15 points but also because of his dribbling, passing, and leaping ability.

"Hank could stay up so long he was like a ballet dancer," his teammate Howie Turner said. "He could fake while driving at a time when people just drove, period. Forty years ago he was making moves that still are considered exceptional today."

East Meets West

Hank Luisetti was ahead of his time—far, far ahead. After his performance at the Garden, the Eastern establishment recognized him for what he was, an innovator who would change the game. Nat Holman agreed that Luisetti was "an amazing marksman, a spectacular dribbler, and a clever passer." Joe Lapchick, another Original Celtic, who had begun coaching at St. John's, was impressed by "his uncanny ability to control the ball while going at top speed." Overnight, kids not only in the East but all over America were shooting basketballs with one hand. Coaches were copying not only Stanford's fast break but also its combination defenses, which used both man-to-man and zone principles. Within a few months the center jump after every basket would be abolished, thereby enabling teams to retaliate quickly.

"I guess we really didn't know what we were starting that night at

Madison Square Garden," Luisetti says. "We had no idea that we would bring on a revolution. And I had no notion of what that one game would mean to me."

Luisetti was named to the All-America team that season and again as a senior. In his final season he set a national collegiate career scoring record with 1,596 points, including 50 against Duquesne in one game. Although the National Basketball League existed then, it was composed mostly of teams in small Midwestern cities, as mentioned previously. Rather than join the NBL, Luisetti preferred to remain in the San Francisco area, where he played for the Olympic Club, an Amateur Athletic Union team. He later played for the Phillips Oilers, another AAU team. Not long after the Japanese attack on Pearl Harbor, he enlisted in the Navy, which stationed him at St. Mary's Pre-Flight School in the San Francisco area. During the 1943–44 season, St. Mary's was undefeated, with Luisetti the high scorer on a team that included Jim Pollard, a Stanford All-America who later was an All-NBA forward with the Minneapolis Lakers.

When World War II ended, Luisetti was only twenty-nine years old, young enough to consider joining one of the new Basketball Association of America teams for the league's first season in 1946. That year the BAA had franchises in Philadelphia, New York, Washington, Boston, Providence, Toronto, Chicago, St. Louis, Cleveland, Detroit, and Pittsburgh. But while awaiting sea duty at Norfolk, Virginia, in 1944, Luisetti had been hospitalized for four months with spinal meningitis. He lost forty pounds. He would never play basketball again, although he coached the Stewart Chevrolet team from San Francisco to the AAU title in 1951.

In those years, AAU basketball represented another career choice for a good college player. Although the NBL's four best teams (Minneapolis, Rochester, Indianapolis, and Fort Wayne) would join the struggling BAA in 1948 to form the NBA, pro basketball did not represent a firm future. Some players preferred the Phillips Oilers of Bartlesville, Oklahoma, who represented the Phillips 66 oil company.

Bob Kurland (left) stretches for a loose ball in the 1952 Olympic trials.

By working for the company in various jobs that would endure beyond their basketball years, the players earned good salaries while maintaining their amateur standing. One of the most successful of AAU players was Bob Kurland, who proved that a 7-foot center could be as coordinated as a smaller athlete.

Nicknamed "Foothills" because of his height, Kurland was a three-time All-America center who led Oklahoma State to the NCAA championship in both 1945 and 1946. He joined the Phillips 66 team, although he considered negotiating with the St. Louis Bombers of the BAA.

"I was all set with Phillips 66," Kurland once said, "but I thought I might like to try my hand as a pro. One day when I was in St. Louis, I stopped by the Bombers' office, but the team was on the road, and there wasn't a single person in the office. I waited around a few minutes, went out for a cup of coffee, and returned. Still there was nobody in the office, so I went on my way. I think I was ready to sign and go pro, but since there was nobody to talk to about it, I still can't be sure. I just went on my way."

His way took the Phillips Oilers to the AAU title and the United States Olympic team to gold medals at London in 1948 and at Helsinki in 1952, just as it had taken Oklahoma State to its two NCAA championships.

"He made our type of game go," said Henry Iba, the Oklahoma State coach. "We knew he would get us the ball, so we never had to rush into a bad shot. And on defense, he not only got rebounds, he blocked shots."

Kurland blocked so many shots, he forced the rule makers to outlaw goaltending. No longer could a player block a shot on its downward path to the basket. Other 7-footers had played college basketball, but most were awkward and slow. Kurland was an athlete. He had been a high jumper, a shot-putter, and a discus thrower. He also worked hard at improving as a basketball player.

"One afternoon he must have tried a hundred hook shots with his left hand," Iba once said. "The first hundred didn't hit either the rim or the backboard; the next hundred didn't go in. But after that, he started to connect."

As an A student who had been the president of the Student Senate at Oklahoma State, Kurland thrived in the AAU atmosphere. At first he stacked oil cans in a Phillips warehouse. But two decades later he was the president of a Phillips subsidiary.

"I may have had some doubts about not going pro," he once acknowledged, "but I don't have to worry about a job. I've got a good one. I've never had any regrets."

George Mikan

No regrets, perhaps, but also nowhere near the recognition Kurland deserved. For all his skill, his decision to play in the AAU rather than pro basketball reduced his stature in the game's history. In an Associated Press balloting of sportswriters in 1950 for the Basketball Player of the Half Century, the 7-foot center received only 4 points. His contemporary, George Mikan, was first with 139 points, and deservedly so. But the three-time All-America center at DePaul had remained much more visible. He signed with the Chicago American Gears for twelve thousand dollars, but when that NBL franchise folded, he joined the Minneapolis Lakers, the National Basketball Association's first dominant team, with five championships in six seasons, primarily because Mikan was the NBA's first dominant center.

Prior to the 1948–49 season, the NBA was formed when the Basketball Association of America absorbed four former National Basketball League franchises—Minneapolis, Rochester, Fort Wayne, and Indianapolis.

In his first three NBA seasons, Mikan won the scoring title with averages of 28.3, 27.4, and 28.4 points a game while the Lakers as a team were averaging fewer than 85 points. In each of his six seasons, he was voted the All-NBA center.

Husky at 6-10 and 245 pounds, Mikan planted himself in the foul lane and relied on his sweeping hook shot. His effectiveness changed the rules. Just as Hank Luisetti had prompted the rule makers to abolish the center jump after each basket and Bob Kurland had prompted them to abolish goaltending, Mikan prompted them to widen the free throw lane. Instead of six feet, the lane was expanded to twelve feet. Not that it stopped Mikan from scoring. Once, when the Lakers were to play the Knicks at Madison Square Garden, the marquee there announced:

Tonight
George Mikan
vs. Knicks

Coached by John Kundla, those Lakers had a balanced team. Jim Pollard and Vern Mikkelsen were the forwards, Slater Martin and Bob Harrison the guards. But after Mikan stopped playing following the 1954 playoffs, the Minneapolis franchise never finished first in the Western Division again. Eventually, in 1960, the franchise was transferred to Los Angeles, the NBA's first California team. Mikan had symbolized the Minneapolis franchise, as he had symbolized DePaul—quite a turnabout for a gangling, bespectacled, stoop-shouldered teenager from Joliet, Illinois, where his parents owned a restaurant and a roller-skating rink.

"Growing up," Mikan once said, "I became so ungainly and so filled with bitterness that my height nearly wrecked my life. I found later that a tall man didn't have to accept clumsiness. He could be well-coordinated and graceful if he was willing to try hard enough to prove himself."

Mikan tried hard, especially after he was rejected by George Keogan, the Notre Dame coach, who called him "too awkward, and besides, he wears glasses." The Notre Dame assistant coach at the time, Ray Meyer, agreed with that assessment. But when Meyer was hired as the head coach at DePaul, he discovered that Mikan had enrolled at the downtown Chicago college. One reason for Mikan's awkwardness, Meyer learned, was a broken leg suffered when he was 5-11 and growing quickly. During some of the time his leg was in a cast, he grew to 6-7 and virtually had to learn how to walk all over again.

To improve Mikan's agility, Meyer had him work against Billy Donato, a 5-5 playmaker, in one-on-one games during practice.

Mikan also skipped rope and shadowboxed. Game by game he developed into a feared basketball player. And with him, DePaul developed into a feared team.

By the end of Mikan's first season, the Blue Demons qualified for the NCAA tournament, which then involved only eight teams, one

George Mikan (99) led the Minneapolis Lakers to five NBA titles.

each from eight geographical areas of the nation. After eliminating Dartmouth, they lost to Georgetown. The following year, 1944, they advanced to the final of the National Invitation Tournament at Madison Square Garden before losing to St. John's. But in 1945, the Blue Demons emerged as the NIT champions, dominating Bowling Green in the final after Mikan had scored 53 points in a 97–53 rout of Rhode Island State in the semifinals. Over Mikan's four seasons, DePaul would have an 81-17 record, a prelude to what he would help the Lakers accomplish in the NBA.

"George Mikan," says Red Auerbach, the Boston Celtics' president and once their coach, "would have been a stickout performer anytime, anywhere, and under any conditions."

The Twenty-four-Second Clock

But in another sense, the dominance of Mikan and the Lakers had weakened the NBA's overall competitive balance. When the Lakers won the 1954 championship series from the Syracuse Nats, the NBA's showcase event displayed two of its small-town franchises, hardly the image it hoped to project to a national audience. As the NBA club owners met following the playoffs, they knew they needed to revive interest. Ironically, the owner of a "small-town" franchise, Danny Biasone of Syracuse, proposed the idea that would revitalize the NBA—the twenty-four-second clock.

No longer was a team able to hold the ball, as the Fort Wayne Pistons had in 1950 against the Lakers for a 19–18 victory, the lowest-scoring game in NBA history. Instead, a team had to get off a shot within twenty-four seconds after it gained possession of the ball. The owners also instituted a team limit on fouls of six per quarter.

With those two rule changes, the NBA finally was off and running, literally. Teams with a good fast break, such as the Boston Celtics with Bob Cousy as their playmaker, suddenly were averaging over one hundred points a game. Throughout the NBA, fans preferred the higher scores. Many of those fans had turned to the NBA following the 1951 point-fixing scandals that involved some of the nation's best college teams—City College of New York (which had swept both the NCAA and NIT titles in 1950, the only school ever to complete that double), Kentucky, Bradley, Long Island University, Manhattan, and Toledo. Several players of All-America stature were implicated—Alex Groza and Ralph Beard of Kentucky, Gene Melchiorre of Bradley, Sherman White of LIU.

Many of the gamblers who had bribed the players sat in the best seats at the Madison Square Garden college doubleheaders, prompting the NCAA to take its national tournament elsewhere. Attendance at Garden doubleheaders dwindled. Except for occasional attractions, it would never be the same there again.

Since then, occasional point-fixing scandals have surfaced in a college-gym atmosphere. But that 1951 scandal rocked basketball the way the 1919 Black Sox scandal had jolted baseball. Babe Ruth has been credited with saving baseball with the popularity of his home runs. And within a few years of the 1951 scandals, basketball had found two saviors.

Arms and the men: Bill Russell and Wilt Chamberlain

Bill Russell and Wilt Chamberlain

*I*NDIVIDUALLY, EACH WAS A TOWERING TALENT. BUT WITHOUT their rivalry, neither might have been so acclaimed. Massive and muscular at 7-1 and 275 pounds, Wilt Chamberlain scored 100 points in an NBA game for the Philadelphia Warriors while averaging 50 points a game that 1961–62 season. Long-armed and quick-handed at 6-10, Bill Russell enabled the Boston Celtics (no relation to the Original Celtics) to dominate the NBA with eleven championships in his thirteen seasons, including eight consecutive titles.

"But only his first year was Wilt a challenge," Russell once said. "Then it became clear that Wilt was great, and I was better."

Russell, of course, was on better teams. But his presence made those Celtic teams better, as Red Auerbach, then the Celtics' coach, thought it would. Russell would be voted the "Greatest Player in NBA History" in 1980 by the Pro Basketball Writers Association of America, but when the NBA teams were awaiting the 1956 draft of college players, Russell had his critics. In leading the University of San Francisco to two NCAA championships and a 55-game winning streak, he had averaged 19.9 points a game as a junior and 21.4 as a senior. Even so, some scouts doubted his ability to shoot against the best NBA centers. Auerbach, however, was not concerned.

"Red recognized," said Eddie Gottlieb, then the Philadelphia Warriors' owner, "that he could take advantage of Russell's defense and rebounding. Red was the first to see what Russell would mean."

Auerbach knew the Celtics needed a commanding center. "Easy Ed" Macauley was a smooth scorer and passer, not a forceful rebounder. But if the Celtics' coach was to draft Russell, he needed to obtain an early choice from another team in a trade. That year the Rochester Royals would draft first, the St. Louis Hawks second. The Royals, who would move to Cincinnati the next year and later to Kansas City and Sacramento as the Kings, were not that interested in Russell for two reasons. One, they already had a powerful rebounder in Maurice Stokes; two, their owner-coach, Lester Harrison, couldn't afford to outbid the Harlem Globetrotters' twenty-five-thousand-dollar offer to Russell.

Auerbach approached the Hawks, offering Macauley, who had been an All-America a decade earlier on St. Louis University's 1949 NIT champions, and Cliff Hagan, a former Kentucky forward who was completing military service.

When the Hawks agreed, the Celtics had the second choice. The day of the 1956 draft, the Royals selected Sihugo Green, an All-America guard from Duquesne; then the Celtics took Russell, even though they knew he wouldn't report until several weeks into the season. Russell was committed to playing in Melbourne, Australia, for the United States Olympic team, which he led to a gold medal.

"I have always operated on the theory that no player is bigger than the team," Auerbach said, "but when you see a player you really want, you should spare no effort in the world to get him."

In his Celtic debut shortly before Christmas that season, Russell scored only 6 points, but he grabbed 16 rebounds. During a fourth-quarter rally, he also blocked three jump shots by Bob Pettit, the Hawks' 6-9 All-NBA forward who had been the scoring champion the previous season. With those blocked shots, the Russell era had begun. One of the first to notice Russell's impact on the game was Macauley, the center the Celtics had traded in order to draft Russell.

"To be a great shooter," Macauley said, "you must be able to concentrate. When you go up for a shot, there can be only one thing on your mind—the hoop. That's where Russell changed things. Now you had two things to concentrate on—the hoop and 'Where is he?' You'd have to stop for just a split second to see where he was. And in that split second, one of his team-mates would catch up to you. Russell's biggest asset was that element of distraction."

Even when Russell didn't block a shot, he often forced a change in its trajectory. To get the ball over Russell's spiderlike arms, a shooter sometimes had to arc it higher than usual, often resulting in a missed shot.

The Celtics' First Title

By the end of Russell's first season, the Celtics had their first championship. Their magical ball-handler, Bob Cousy, was the NBA's best playmaker as well as one of its most dangerous clutch scorers. Their other guard, Bill Sharman, was the NBA's best shooter. At forward they had Jim Loscutoff, a rugged rebounder, and Tom Heinsohn, a rookie forward from Holy Cross chosen in the "territorial draft" that at the

With Bill Russell at center, the University of San Francisco and the Celtics ruled the boards.

time enabled a franchise to select a popular player from a nearby college. The "sixth man," a position Auerbach would create, was Frank Ramsey, who could play either forward or guard. As the years progressed, the Celtics would add John Havlicek, a sixth man at first and then an All-NBA forward; K. C. Jones, a defensive guard who would coach the Celtics to their 1984 and 1986 championships; Sam Jones, one of the NBA's most accurate shooters; Don Nelson, a hard-working forward; and Tom "Satch" Sanders, a forward who concentrated mostly on defense. But no matter who his teammates were, Russell was the difference, a five-time winner of the Most Valuable Player Award.

"Russell makes up for a lot of mistakes his teammates make," said Eddie Donovan, the Knicks' coach during much of the Russell era. "He protects them. No one goes down the middle against Russell; he forces you to change your offense. And his great ability to move at the last second is the reason he so seldom commits a foul."

Not that Russell was helpless on offense. Over his career he averaged 15.1 points a game, with a high of 18.9 during the 1961–62 season. In the playoffs, he averaged 16.2 points a game, with a high of 22.4 in 1962. But perhaps his most significant statistic is 4,104 rebounds in the playoffs, an NBA record average of 24.8 a game. Year after year, Russell dominated the NBA playoffs more than any other athlete has in postseason competition in any other sport.

Beginning with the 1957 playoffs through the 1969 playoffs, the Celtics won every year but 1958, when Russell hobbled through the championship series on a sprained ankle, and 1967, when he was completing his first of three seasons as Auerbach's successor as coach while still playing.

Russell was the first black man to coach an NBA team, nearly a decade before baseball's first black manager, Frank Robinson of the Cleveland Indians, and at a time when the National Football League had hardly any black assistant coaches. But when Auerbach first asked Russell if he would be interested in the job, Russell had a question.

"Do you really want me, Red?" Russell asked. "Or is this just a token gesture?"

"I never made a token gesture in my life," Auerbach said. "I asked you, didn't I?"

Russell took the job. He would emerge as the only player-coach of an NBA championship team, in both 1968 and 1969, but 1967 was Wilt Chamberlain's year to be on a championship team for the first time. Wilt later would be with the 1972 champions, the Los Angeles Lakers, but in 1967 he was able to help dethrone the Celtics and his nemesis, Russell, who had prevented him from being on a title team in earlier years. The same season that Russell joined the Celtics, Chamberlain was averaging 29.6 points a game as a University of Kansas sophomore, but in the NCAA final, the Jayhawks would lose to North Carolina, 54–53, in triple overtime.

"We just surrounded Wilt," explained Frank McGuire, the North Carolina coach. "Whenever he got the ball, we were all over him."

The next season, other teams tried that same strategy. Not that it helped. Wilt averaged 30.1 points a game, but then he decided to drop out of college rather than subject himself to being surrounded by opposing players in every game, a giraffe hounded by jackals. Ineligible for the NBA draft, he spent a season touring with the Harlem Globetrotters before he was selected in 1959 by the Philadelphia Warriors as their special territorial choice because he had grown up there. Nobody else in NBA history ever broke in the way Wilt did—not George Mikan or Bill Russell before him, not Kareem Abdul-Jabbar or Larry Bird or Magic Johnson or Michael Jordan after him. As a rookie Wilt led the NBA with a 37.6 scoring average and a 26.9 rebounding average. His second season, he improved—38.4 scoring average, a 27.2 rebounding average.

Averaging 50.4 Points a Game

But his third season is the one chiseled into history. He averaged 50.4 points a game. He scored 100 points in a 169–147 victory over the Knicks on March 2, 1962, at Hershey, Pennsylvania, where the Warriors occasionally played a home game. That night he shot 36 of 63 from the floor, 28 of 32 from the free throw line.

"It wasn't my most artistic game," Chamberlain has said. "I could have shot better, even though I impressed myself with my foul shooting. And the game itself, not just my part in it, was not particularly artistic. There were so many bad shots in the last quarter when the

game got to be a real farce. After I broke the record of 78 points, which I set earlier that season, the Knicks decided they didn't want someone to score 100 points against them. The Knicks started to do anything they could to prevent me from getting 100 points. They'd foul my teammates intentionally so the ball wouldn't come to me. But they couldn't get the ball from Guy Rodgers, he was so fast. They couldn't even foul him. And when the ball got to me, they'd foul me immediately. They wouldn't even try to stop me. Just foul me and hope I missed the foul shots, but I didn't miss many. Down at the other end, the Knicks wouldn't shoot. They held the ball as long as they could to keep me from getting it. When I realized they didn't want me to score 100, that served as my motivation."

When the final quarter began, Wilt needed 31 points. He had opened with 23 in the first quarter and 18 in the second for a total of 41 at halftime, then added 28 in the third quarter. That night he also had 25 rebounds.

"Before Wilt scored 100 that night," said Frank McGuire, the former North Carolina coach who was his Warrior coach that season, "I never thought it was out of the realm of possibility for him. He could do whatever he wanted to do on a basketball court, or anywhere else for that matter. If he wanted to score 100 or even more, if he wanted 50 rebounds, or 30 blocked shots, or 20 assists, he'd get them. No one player, not even Bill Russell, could stop him."

In that year's playoffs Wilt averaged 35 points and 26 rebounds as the Warriors extended the Celtics to a decisive seventh game in the Eastern Division final before losing, 109–107.

"Wilt played hard, he played hurt," McGuire said. "He took a lot of abuse, physical and verbal. It's like some people didn't realize what he was giving them. He had the greatest season ever by an NBA player, but some people knocked him because we didn't win the league championship. The Celtics had superior personnel, but they didn't have anyone like Wilt. No one did."

For the 1962–63 season, the Warrior franchise moved to San Francisco and Wilt's scoring average *dropped* to 44.8 points on a team with a 31-49 record. But then the Warriors changed coaches, hiring Alex Hannum, who changed Wilt's game.

"For us to win," Hannum said, "Wilt has to play like Bill Russell when we're on defense and play like Wilt Chamberlain when we're on offense. And he's done it. I didn't have any trouble getting Wilt to do what I wanted him to do on defense."

All those seasons of frustration in not being on a title team persuaded Wilt to try it Hannum's way. But during the 1964–65 season Wilt was traded back to Philadelphia, where the transfer of the Syracuse Nats had created the 76er franchise. Prior to the 1966–67 season, the 76ers hired Hannum as their new coach.

"I don't care about my points," Wilt kept saying in those years. "All I care about is winning the NBA championship."

In the 1967 playoffs, his 76ers won the championship. Wilt had averaged 24 points per game as the 76ers ruled the regular season with a 65-13 record. In the playoffs, they dethroned the Celtics, four games to one, in the Eastern Division final, then eliminated the San Francisco Warriors in six games for the title. Wilt finally had his championship ring. But when the 76ers, after holding a 3–1 lead, were dethroned by the Celtics in the Eastern final the following year, Wilt was traded again, this time to the Los Angeles Lakers.

"Everybody pulls for David, nobody roots for Goliath," Wilt once said. "My entire career, I've been blamed for the failures of others."

Before the Los Angeles Lakers finally won their first championship in 1972, they soared into those playoffs after a record thirty-three-game winning streak. And in the title series, Wilt enjoyed his finest hour. In the fifth game, he finished off the Knicks with 24 points, 29 rebounds, and 10 blocked shots in a 114–100 victory while playing with a broken right wrist. X rays the previous day had disclosed the fracture. Wilt secretly treated the wrist with ice packs and whirlpool baths to reduce the swelling. In the dressing room before the final game, Wilt handled the ball—palming it, throwing it, catching it. Although his wrist had enough flexibility for him to play, he wore a padded wrap on it. As he celebrated later with orange juice, he still wore the wrap.

"Nothing greater, that's how I feel," he said. "When we beat the Celtics five years ago, we were picked. This one is the most satisfying. For a long while, me and friends of mine, we'd hear, 'Wilt can't win the big ones, this team can't win the big ones!'"

The Sixty-three-Foot Shot

Wilt had exorcised his demons. So had all the other Lakers, especially Jerry West, their 6-3 guard from West Virginia, who had been on seven Laker teams that lost the title series—six times to the Celtics and once to the Knicks in 1970—when he scored the most memorable single basket in NBA history. With the Knicks leading, 102–100, after a jump shot by Dave DeBusschere, only three seconds remained on the clock as Chamberlain quickly threw the ball inbounds to West to the left of the foul lane. West dribbled three times, moving to the right to avoid Willis Reed, and took two steps beyond the free throw circle. From about sixty-three feet away, he let fly a one-hander.

"He looked so determined," Walt Frazier, the Knicks' guard, said later. "He thought it was really going to go in."

It did. Watching from under the basket, DeBusschere was so shocked, he toppled backward onto the floor. Chamberlain was so shocked, he thought the Lakers had won. He tousled West's hair, then hurried toward the locker room. West knew better.

"I knew we still had to play overtime," he said later. "If the shot had ended the game, it would have felt great."

Instead, the Lakers lost, 111–108, and they would lose that series in seven games. But win or lose, Jerry West was considered to be basketball's best clutch shooter.

"If it comes down to one shot, I like to shoot the ball," he said. "I don't worry about it. If it doesn't go in, it doesn't go in."

It went in often enough for West to rank first among NBA play-off scorers with a 29.1 average and to rank third among regular-season career scorers with a 27-point average, behind Wilt

Jerry West (44) averaged 29.1 points in the NBA playoffs.

Chamberlain and Elgin Baylor, his Laker teammate for more than a decade. Smooth and supple, the 6-5 Baylor didn't last long enough to share the 1972 championship, but perhaps no other player enjoyed the game so much.

"The traveling, the schedule, the crazy hours have never bothered me," Baylor once said. "I hear players younger than I am saying that they can't get up for games anymore. I don't know what they're talking about. The day I decide to retire, it probably will be because I've had a whole season where I could not shake a succession of lingering injuries."

The Big O

Knee problems eventually forced Baylor to retire without the championship ring that he deserved. His misfortune was having to go up against the Celtics so often in the title round, just as it was Oscar Robertson's misfortune to be on the Cincinnati Royals during the same decade. Now when an NBA player achieves a "triple double," meaning double figures in points, rebounds, and assists in one game, it rates headlines. In 1962 "the Big O" *averaged* a triple double for the season—30.8 points, 12.5 rebounds, and 11.4 assists. For all that, his teammates' talent was too thin for the Royals to win a championship. But in 1970 the Big O was traded to the Milwaukee Bucks, who needed a wise head in the backcourt to guide their young 7-2 center, Lew Alcindor (who later changed his name to Kareem Abdul-Jabbar). In the Big O's first season there, the Bucks qualified for the playoff final against the Baltimore Bullets.

"We'll do what we've done all season," Robertson said before that series began. "We'll work inside with Lew, we'll run, we'll keep the ball moving."

In a rare sweep, the Bucks won in four games. In fourteen playoff games that year, the Big O averaged 18 points, a reminder of his dazzling seasons with the Royals, when he had a reputation of being able to get off a good shot no matter what player was covering him. If he couldn't fake a defender out of position, he could muscle his way past. Even if a much taller player tried to stop him near the basket, he would fake the taller player into going up and down. When the taller player eventually was coming down, the Big O would be going up for two points.

"But the thing about Oscar," Tom Heinsohn, then with the Celtics and later a television analyst, once said, "is that he knows all phases of the game—passing, shooting, rebounding. If you double-team him, that calls for him to pass. And he'll pass it."

On the Bucks, of course, the Big O was passing the ball to the center who would develop into the NBA's all-time leading scorer. Kareem Abdul-Jabbar would dominate the NBA, just as he had dominated college basketball at UCLA during the John Wooden regime.

Oscar Robertson somehow always got off a good shot.

John Wooden's UCLA Dynasty

WHEN A UCLA GAME WAS ABOUT TO BEGIN, JOHN WOODEN turned to where his wife, Nell, was sitting and winked at her. He patted the knee of the assistant coach next to him. He bent down and pulled up his socks. He leaned over to tap the floor. He reached into the left pocket of his jacket and fingered a small silver crucifix. Then he picked up a rolled program, occasionally waving it during the game as if he were conducting an orchestra. And in a sense he was directing an orchestra that produced symphonies of success.

At the end of ten seasons, those symphonies created another ritual for the UCLA coach—accepting the NCAA championship trophy.

In the American sports scene, college basketball's Final Four now ranks in importance with baseball's World Series, pro football's Super Bowl, and the NBA championship series. Of all the college

John Wooden coached ten NCAA championship teams at UCLA.

coaches, nobody did as much as John Wooden in raising the stature of the Final Four, meaning the four teams that qualify for the national semifinals from the regional tournaments. His UCLA teams won those ten championships, including seven in a row, over a span of only twelve seasons, beginning in 1964 and ending in 1975, when he announced that the title game would be his last as a coach.

Although the Boston Celtics won eleven NBA titles in thirteen years, many basketball people consider UCLA's feat even more remarkable. Throughout the Celtics' reign, Bill Russell was a constant at center. Several other All-NBA players, notably Bob Cousy and John Havlicek, were on six of those title teams. Perhaps even more important, the Celtics could lose a game or two, even three, in a playoff series and go on to win it. In the NCAA tournament, after one loss a team is eliminated. And at UCLA, as at all colleges, the natural turnover of personnel required Wooden to adjust each season.

John Havlicek (17) played on six Celtic championship teams.

The arrival of Lew Alcindor, now known as Kareem Abdul-Jabbar, launched UCLA on a streak of seven consecutive championship teams, although the 7-2 center was on only the first three.

"You get a good run of players, a dominant player like Alcindor, and people say you're supposed to win three championships, and we did," Wooden once said. "But Ohio State was supposed to win three with Jerry Lucas and John Havlicek and that bunch, and it won only one. Kansas was supposed to win three with Wilt Chamberlain, and one year they didn't even win their conference championship. We were supposed to do it. And we did it. For the most part, we've done what we're supposed to do. There's no way you can have consistent success without players. No one can win without material. But not everyone can win with material."

With "material," John Wooden won more NCAA titles than any other college basketball coach. And that's the test of any coach, no matter what the sport, no matter what the level of the sport.

In his twenty-seven seasons at the University of California, Los Angeles, his won-lost record was 620-147, a remarkable .804 winning percentage. But he didn't create much impact nationally until 1964, when UCLA won its first NCAA title in his sixteenth season there. Until then, he had a provincial reputation at UCLA, and he

John Wooden won three national championships with Lew Alcindor (later Kareem Abdul-Jabbar).

remained a legend in Indiana as a three-time All-America guard at Purdue and that state's best high-school guard until Oscar Robertson arrived. But fate twice preserved Wooden for his task of lifting UCLA to national prominence.

While in the Navy during World War II as a physical education instructor, Wooden received orders to serve on the aircraft carrier *Franklin* in the South Pacific. But when he needed an emergency appendectomy, his orders were canceled. As he recuperated, a Japanese kamikaze plane exploded on the *Franklin*, killing many naval personnel, including the officer who had replaced him on the ship's roster.

After two seasons as the Indiana State coach, Wooden was being pursued in 1948 by both UCLA and Minnesota when a blizzard prevented Minnesota officials from phoning him with an offer he might have accepted. Having not heard from the Minnesota people by the appointed hour, the man that Kareem Abdul-Jabbar's mother described as "more like a minister than a coach" accepted the UCLA offer.

"You Are Here for an Education"

With his close-cropped hair, horn-rimmed glasses, and face of a Midwestern farmer, Wooden projected the image of the deacon he was at the First Christian Church of Santa Monica, not far from the UCLA campus. He spoke softly but firmly. Always keeping his role in perspective, he often reminded his players, "You are here for an education. That comes first. Basketball comes second." But at practice and during games, he taught basketball as if it were a religion.

"I am not a strategic coach," he once said. "I am a practice coach."

Wooden emphasized the fundamentals of basketball, but he also emphasized the fundamentals of life. To each of his UCLA players, he would pass out a copy of his "pyramid of success." The pyramid's foundation is built on industriousness, friendship, loyalty, cooperation, and enthusiasm. Above is a layer of self-control, alertness, initiative, and intentness. Additional layers of condition, skill, team spirit, poise, confidence, and competitive greatness are surrounded by sloping walls of ambition, adaptability, resourcefulness, fight, faith, patience, reliability, integrity, honesty, and sincerity. All these attributes support "success" at the pinnacle of the pyramid.

"Success," the UCLA coach once said, "is the peace of mind that is a direct result of the self-satisfaction in knowing you did your best to become the best that you are capable of becoming."

In addition to winning 10 NCAA championships, Wooden's teams had two spectacular winning streaks—one of 88 games that ended in 1974, another of 47 games that ended in 1968. But win or lose, their coach never reacted emotionally.

"I don't like emotion," he often said. "Emotion leads to peaks and valleys, and I don't like valleys."

Wooden also did not rely on pep talks. Before the 1964 championship game against Duke, he tested his players' memory with a question.

"Who can remember," the coach asked, "which team finished second in the NCAA tournament two years ago?"

When none of his players knew the answer, Wooden had impressed upon them the importance of not wasting the opportunity to be a championship team, rather than a quickly forgotten runner-up team. That night the Bruins won, 98–83, completing a 30-0 season with Walt Hazzard, who became the UCLA coach two decades later, as their playmaker. Alongside him was a baby-faced 6-1 guard, Gail Goodrich, who would lead the Bruins to their 1965 championship with 42 points in a 91–80 victory over Michigan.

Even with successive championship teams, Wooden did not yet attain the stature of several other college coaches, notably Adolph Rupp, whose Kentucky teams had won the NCAA title in 1948, 1949, 1951, and 1958. In the 1966 tournament, Kentucky appeared ready to win another championship when it opposed Texas Western (now known as the University of Texas at El Paso) in the final, but Rupp's team lost, 72–65.

Texas Western was ahead of its time. Coach Don Haskins' five starters and his first two players off the bench were black—Bobby Joe Hill, Orsten Artis, David "Big Daddy" Lattin, Harry Flournoy, Willie Worsley (a 5-6 sophomore who could dunk), Nevil Shed, and Willie Cager. Although the Miners were relatively unknown before that Final Four, they stunned Kentucky with fundamental basketball, especially a man-to-man defense that forced the Wildcats into costly turnovers. Sociologically, the Miners also changed the minds of Rupp and other college coaches, especially in the South, who had resisted racial integration.

"All I did was play my best people," Haskins said on his election to the Basketball Hall of Fame in 1997. "It was that simple."

Adolph Rupp's Kentucky teams won four NCAA titles.

Lew Alcindor Arrives

Wooden had realized the value of black players years before. Even as Texas Western was winning the NCAA title, Wooden was looking ahead to UCLA's first season with Lew Alcindor, who had not played on the varsity as a freshman in accordance with the NCAA rules of that era.

In his varsity opener, Alcindor scored 56 points, prompting Wooden to describe him as "awesome." The only child of a 6-2 New York Transit Authority policeman and a 6-0 light-opera singer, Alcindor grew up in New York City, leading Power Memorial Academy to three Catholic High School Athletic Association titles with a 95-6 record. During his senior year, he narrowed his college choices to a few teams, but Wooden asked a favor of Jack Donohue, the Power coach.

"When Lewis goes around visiting colleges," Wooden said, "please have him come to UCLA last."

Wooden knew that the last college a player visits usually leaves a stronger impression than those of the campuses he saw earlier. The coach also knew the UCLA's new five-million-dollar athletic center, Pauley Pavilion, would be nearer completion. Not long after Alcindor's visit, he enrolled there.

"I chose UCLA," he explained, "because it has the atmosphere I wanted and because the people out there were very nice to me."

Alcindor, in turn, would be very nice to UCLA's basketball atmosphere. During Alcindor's sophomore season, the Bruins were undefeated entering the Final Four, where they would oppose Houston, with Elvin Hayes, in the semifinals. "No way Lew's gonna run over me," Hayes said defiantly. Hayes was correct. Hayes outscored Alcindor, 25–19, and outrebounded him, 24–20, but after Alcindor blocked Hayes's dunk attempt midway in the first half, the Bruins took command, winning, 73–58. In the final they toyed with Dayton, 79–64.

Midway through the next season, the Alcindor-Hayes rivalry flared again. UCLA took its 47-game winning streak to the Houston Astrodome, where 52,693 spectators saw the Cougars win, 71–69. Alcindor had only 15 points, scoring on only 4 of 18 shots, and only 12 rebounds, but in his previous game he had suffered a scratched eyeball.

"No, my eyes didn't bother me," he said later, "but I didn't feel physically right."

Two months later, awaiting a Final Four rematch, Alcindor felt better. Wooden, meanwhile, had decided to use a special defense—the "diamond and one"—in hopes of stopping Hayes. Whenever the Cougars had the ball, four UCLA players formed a diamond-shaped zone defense. One lined up beyond the top of the foul circle, two on opposite sides of the circle, one under the basket. The fifth UCLA defender, Lynn Shackleford, followed Hayes wherever he went. Hayes scored 10 points as UCLA won, 101–69.

In the title game, Alcindor scored 34 points in a 78–55 rout of North Carolina, but the Houston game had been sweeter for the UCLA players.

For three
seasons, UCLA
stood for the
University of
California,
Lew Alcindor.

"They'd had a lot to say about us, but I don't think they were correct," Alcindor said. "We wanted to teach those people some manners."

The next year, Alcindor's final season, UCLA emerged as the first college to win three consecutive NCAA championships, with a 92–72 victory over Purdue. As the only three-time Most Valuable Player in Final Four history, Alcindor helped the Bruins complete an 88-2 record over his three seasons. In addition to the loss to Houston, the Bruins were surprised by Southern Cal, 46–44, midway through his final season.

But when Alcindor departed to join the Milwaukee Bucks, the question was: Can the UCLA Bruins and John Wooden go on winning NCAA championships without the center who soon would be known as Kareem Abdul-Jabbar?

UCLA answered that question by extending its streak of titles to seven, then adding another in Wooden's final season for a total of ten.

Sidney Wicks, Curtis Rowe, Steve Patterson, and Henry Bibby led the Bruins to their 1970 championship, an 80–69 victory over Jacksonville, which had Artis Gilmore, a 7-2 center. The next year, they defeated Villanova, 68–62, for the title, completing a 27-1 record disrupted only by an 89–82 loss at Notre Dame when Austin Carr scored 46 points. Wicks and Rowe departed, but by then Bill Walton, a rangy 6-11 redheaded center, had arrived. During the 1971–72 season, the Bruins swept through thirty games, including an 81–76 triumph over Florida State for the NCAA title. Their average margin of victory was an astounding 33 points.

"I've never seen a shot-blocker the equal of Bill Russell," Wooden said, "but imagine what Walton would do if he were playing under the same rules Russell did in college, with the narrower lane and the absence of basket-interference rules."

Walton was equally effective on offense. When the Bruins dominated Memphis State, 87–66, for the 1973 title, he scored 44 points, hitting on 21 of his 22 field-goal attempts, each a championship-game record. In Walton's final season, 1973–74, the Bruins were

Swooping
high, Bill
Walton led
UCLA to two
NCAA titles.

expected to sweep to another title. But in January, their eighty-eight-game winning streak ended at Notre Dame; and in the Final Four, they were upset by North Carolina State, 80–77, in two overtimes. The following year, as a good-bye present to Wooden, the Bruins captured the title again with a 92–85 victory over Kentucky following a 75–74 squeaker in overtime with Louisville, coached by Denny Crum, who had been Wooden's top assistant coach.

To the end Wooden remained the master, the professor who was still smarter than his brightest pupil.

"I'm proud of the fact that I won championships with different types of teams," Wooden said. "We won three with Kareem and two with Bill Walton, but those were only five of the ten. We won in 1964 without a starter taller than 6-5. We won in 1970 and 1971 without a dominating center, and we won in 1975 with a pair of guards [Andre McCarter and Pete Trgovich] a lot of people thought would be our downfall. If I'm to be remembered as a great coach, I think it should be because I won with so many different types of teams."

Discipline and Control

Wooden also won with different types of personalities in an era of protest on many college campuses.

"I was brought up believing in discipline, in control, and I demanded those things when I coached," Wooden said. "Some of my players didn't care for that approach, but I didn't expect them to. They were young, and the young naturally rebel against discipline. They didn't have to like it. But they did have to accept it, or at least adapt to it, if they wanted to play for me. I didn't treat all the players alike. I sought to give them the treatment they earned, deserved, or responded to. I can't say I liked them all equally; nor did all the players like each other. Yet all that should be forgotten on the floor."

To appreciate what Wooden accomplished in coaching ten championship teams, consider that Kentucky is next with six titles. His seven consecutive championship teams are put in perspective when you consider that only Duke has won even two consecutive titles since he stopped coaching and that only four other colleges have won as many as two consecutive championships since the NCAA tournament began in 1939—Oklahoma State, Kentucky, San Francisco, and Cincinnati. Wooden's four teams with unbeaten seasons—those of 1964, 1967, 1972, and 1973—set another record that is not likely to be equaled, or even approached.

UCLA and John Wooden established the Final Four as one of America's premier sports events, so much so that when the Bruins were no longer a dominant team, the Final Four developed even more importance than it had when Wooden's teams were winning ten titles. And in 1979 the Final Four would feature two players who would go on to dominate the NBA—Larry Bird of Indiana State and Earvin "Magic" Johnson of Michigan State.

MODERN TIMES

Michael Jordan

OUTSIDE THE MAIN ENTRANCE TO THE UNITED CENTER IN Chicago, the huge bronze statue shows him in full flight with a basketball. Underneath, the inscription on a plaque reads:

> Michael Jordan
> Chicago Bulls
> 1984–1993
> The best there ever was. The best there ever will be.

As definitive as those superlatives are, they create virtually no argument among basketball followers. But the time frame is incomplete. When that statue was erected, Michael Jordan had stopped playing for the three-time NBA champion Chicago Bulls in order to be a minor-league baseball outfielder. But, as if to justify the words in the inscription, "The Best" not only rejoined the Bulls but led what is arguably the best basketball team ever to the 1996 title.

As spectacular as he had been in his first tenure with the Bulls, he was in some ways even better in his comeback.

When he was voted his fourth Most Valuable Player award in 1996, he called it "more meaningful" than the others. "I learned a lesson," he said, thinking of the 1995 playoffs when the Bulls were eliminated by the Orlando Magic in the Eastern Conference Finals. "That no matter how great you were before you left, you just can't come back and turn it on."

Motivated by the embarrassment of that six-game playoff loss, "The Best There Ever Was" dedicated himself at age thirty-two to scraping off what little rust had formed on his skills during his seventeen-month absence from pro basketball.

Embarrassment has always inspired Jordan. As a sophomore at Emsley Laney High School in Wilmington, North Carolina, he was cut from the varsity tryouts. Instead of getting discouraged, he got better. And better.

When the Bulls regrouped for the 1995–96 schedule, not only was Jordan better, but the entire team was better too. Its 72-10 record was the best in NBA history, surpassing the 69-13 record of the Los Angeles Lakers with Wilt Chamberlain and Jerry West during the 1971–72 season. Jordan did not do it alone. In basketball no one player ever does, not even this 6-5 shooting guard.

"I've never seen three guys," he said that season, meaning forward Scottie Pippen, rebounder Dennis Rodman, and himself, "who excel at three different things the way we do."

In his earlier years Jordan often scored on soaring slam dunks after driving to the basket. But in the 1996–97 season he led the NBA in scoring for a record ninth time after developing a deadly turnaround jump shot.

"The two shots are very similar," he said. "In each case, you're demoralizing the defense when they felt they've got you under control."

Jordan's understanding of the opposing defense's reaction is another example of his genius. For all his points and passes, for all his dunks and dramatics, he also earned a reputation as one of the NBA's best defensive players, especially in the final minutes of a close game.

"If one particular player was hot," said Johnny Bach, the Bulls' assistant coach for defense on their first three title teams, "You could say, 'Michael, take him out of the game for us.'"

The Dream Team

No opposing player ever took Michael Jordan out of the game. As a University of North Carolina freshman, he scored the winning basket for the Tar Heels in their 63–62 victory over Georgetown for the 1982 NCAA title. In 1984, shortly after being chosen by the Bulls as the third choice in the NBA draft, he was on the U.S. Olympic gold medal basketball team. In 1992 he earned another gold medal with the original Dream Team, mostly NBA players.

Until then the U.S. Olympic team was composed of college players about to join NBA teams, as Jordan had been in 1984, but after the 1988 team had finished fourth in Seoul, the Olympic rules were changed to allow NBA players to compete for their home nation.

In addition to Jordan, that original Dream Team, which was coached by Chuck Daly, featured the NBA's best: Earvin "Magic" Johnson, Larry Bird, Patrick Ewing, David Robinson, Charles Barkley, Karl Malone, Chris Mullin, Scottie Pippen, Clyde Drexler, John Stockton, and Christian Laettner.

Wearing their Olympic gold medals, the 1992 Dream Team watches the raising of the flag at Barcelona.

Michael Jordan also symbolized the growth of the NBA as a threat to both football and baseball as America's most popular sport. His $30 million salary for the 1996–97 schedule was a record one-season amount for an athlete in a team sport. His worldwide celebrity brought him millions more in commercials and endorsements. His stature helped the NBA expand to a conglomerate featuring NBA

Properties, NBA Entertainment, NBA Television and New Media Ventures, and the Women's NBA. Jordan's magnitude was such that Grant Hill, touted by some observers as the eventual successor to "The Best There Ever Was," respectfully declined to endorse the comparison.

"No matter how much people talk about my athletic ability," Hill said during his third season with the Detroit Pistons, "I don't have the hand size to do what Michael does with the ball when he's in the air. And I don't have nearly his ability to elevate above people when I go to the hoop."

Even so, the 6-8 Hill was building a sturdy résumé—instant All-Star forward, member of the 1996 Olympic Dream Team, two NCAA championships while at Duke University. Plus the willingness to lead his teammates.

"Criticism comes with being a leader," Hill said. "It's like being a quarterback. When things go well, you get a lot of the credit. When things go wrong, you get a lot of the blame. Am I ready to deal with that? Yes, because I want to win, and I want to be a top player. That means you put yourself out there and hold yourself accountable. That's what I'm trying to do. And, hopefully, that attitude will help me get a ring, or two, or three, before I'm through."

He meant the NBA championship ring that every player aspires to as a symbol of stature—the ring that Magic Johnson and Larry Bird won so often.

Magic Johnson and Larry Bird were the old pros of the original Dream Team, each so different yet so alike, their careers forever intertwined. For Johnson, basketball was fun and high-fives, always with a smile. For Bird, it was a blue-collar job, with seldom a smile. But the essence of each was the same.

"The number one thing is desire," Bird said, "the ability to do the things you have to do to become a basketball player. I don't think you can teach anyone desire. I think it's a gift. I don't know why I have it, but I do."

That gift was obvious when the Boston Celtics' 6-9 forward

hustled for a rebound or for a loose ball. It was even more obvious when he was at home in French Lick, Indiana, during the off-season. After a pickup game on his backyard court, he stayed out there by himself, shooting.

"Say you're playing basketball for an hour and a half, three on three," Bird said. "During that time you'll take maybe a hundred shots. But if you go out by yourself for an hour and a half, you can take a thousand shots. Maybe more. From anywhere you want."

"Reckless and Abandon"

Magic Johnson had that same gift, that same desire. But with him, it showed in his smile, in his voice, in his vocabulary. "It's winnin' time," he would say. Or he talked about how he "strives on pressure." And when the 6-9 guard rejoined the Los Angeles Lakers after knee surgery, he wasn't concerned that he might perform timidly.

"I only know how to play two ways," he said. "That's reckless and abandon."

Magic would be on five Laker championship teams, but at age thirty-two, his career was suddenly interrupted. Shortly before the 1991–92 season was about to begin, he announced that he had contracted the virus that causes the dreaded disease AIDS. He returned to play in the All-Star

Magic Johnson floats to the basket for another two points.

game that season and was a member of the 1992 Olympic Dream Team but changed his mind about a 1992 comeback when some opposing players voiced concern about playing against him because of his virus. He coached the Lakers briefly in 1995, then rejoined them as a player early in 1996, retiring after the playoffs.

"It's time to move on," he said. "I'm going out on my terms, something I couldn't say when I aborted a comeback in 1992."

As a Laker rookie in the 1980 playoffs, Magic quickly earned a NBA championship ring. During the season he had averaged 18 points a game while ranking seventh in assists and fifth in steals. As a point guard, his job was to get the ball to Kareem Abdul-Jabbar, the 7-2 center with the sky hook. But against the 76ers in the fifth game of the championship playoff series, Abdul-Jabbar wrenched his left ankle late in the third quarter. He would return to finish with 40 points in a 108–103 victory that provided the Lakers with a 3–2 lead in the series. The next morning his ankle was swollen. When the Lakers went to Philadelphia for the sixth game, Abdul-Jabbar remained in Los Angeles, hoping he would recuperate for a decisive seventh game there. But that created a big question for Paul Westhead, the Lakers' coach.

"Who's your center?" he was asked.

"Magic," the coach said with a smile.

Some reporters thought Westhead was joking, but the coach explained that Magic not only was an agile 6-9 but had played center in high school. At the opening whistle, Magic jumped center and drifted into the high post. At times he reverted to his usual position, point guard or playmaker, and occasionally he was a shooting guard, a power forward, and a small forward. When the Lakers completed their 123–107 victory, he had 42 points with 15 rebounds, 7 assists, 3 steals, and a blocked shot—one of the most spectacular individual efforts in NBA playoff history.

"Magic thinks every season goes like that," Westhead said. "You play some games, win the title, and get named MVP."

That year, and again two years later, the 76ers couldn't quite handle the Lakers in the championship playoff, but 1983 would be the 76ers' year. In order to cope with Abdul-Jabbar, the 76ers had obtained Moses Malone, a workhorse scorer and rebounder in a trade with the Houston Rockets. When the 76ers were about to enter the playoffs after notching a 65-17 record during the regular season, Malone was asked to assess their chances in the playoffs.

"Four, four, and four," he said.

Doctor J

His prediction missed by one game. The 76ers swept the Knicks in four games, eliminated the Milwaukee Bucks in five games for the Eastern Conference title, then swept the Lakers for the championship. Malone averaged 24.5 points and 15.3 rebounds that season, but the final game of the title series belonged to Julius Erving, the 6-7 forward known as "Doctor J," the designer of the soaring slam dunk. During a time-out with the 76ers trailing, 106–104, the Doctor quietly addressed his teammates.

"I'm taking over," he said.

Quickly the Doctor stole a Laker pass and dunked. Moments later he swooped in for another basket, then added a free throw. The next time the 76ers got the ball, he tossed in a one-hander over Magic Johnson from the top of the foul circle. The 76ers went on to win, 115–108. The Doctor indeed had taken over as he had in so many games for the New York Nets of the rival American Basketball Association (ABA) earlier in his career. Erving had gotten his nickname while growing up on Long Island in Roosevelt, New York. He once talked about studying to be a doctor someday, and his friends began calling him "Doctor," which developed into "Doctor J."

"There are athletes who are known as 'the franchise,'" said Dave DeBusschere, the commissioner who had been on two NBA championship teams as a Knick forward, "but Julius isn't the franchise—he's the league."

In his years
with the Nets,
Doctor J
symbolized
the ABA itself.

The ABA had been formed in 1967. In an attempt to attract fans to the fledgling league, the owners established a three-point shot from beyond twenty-three feet nine inches, which the NBA later adopted. The ABA also sported a red, white, and blue ball, which the NBA did not adopt. "That ball," Alex Hannum, a longtime NBA coach, once said, "belongs on the nose of a seal." But until the NBA absorbed four teams (the New York Nets, Denver Nuggets, Indiana Pacers, and San Antonio Spurs) in 1976, that ball was handled by some of basketball's best players, notably Doctor J, Artis Gilmore, George "Iceman" Gervin, Dan Issel, Rick Barry, David Thompson, George McGinnis, Bobby Jones, and Moses Malone, then a teenager who decided to join the Utah Stars rather than enroll at the University of Maryland.

More than any other player, Doctor J symbolized the ABA, especially after he was traded to the Nets by the Virginia Squires, who had signed him in 1971 following his sophomore season at the University of Massachusetts.

Some people wondered if the Doctor was really as good as his ABA record. Over his five seasons he had averaged 31.3 points a game while leading the Nets to the 1974 and 1976 titles. Not that he had any doubts about himself. Asked once if he thought he could be as effective in the NBA as he was in the ABA, he never hesitated.

"Yup," he said, quietly but firmly.

Traded to the 76ers in 1976, shortly after the NBA absorbed the four ABA franchises, the Doctor proved his "Yup" to be an understatement. Averaging more than 20 points a game for nine seasons, he was named to the All-NBA team five times. The day before the 1983 All-Star Game, he was showing his two young sons the game's MVP trophy, which he had won six years earlier, during his first NBA season.

"Did you win that, Daddy?" one asked.

"Not lately," the Doctor said, smiling.

"Well, you bring that trophy home," the boy said.

"I'll try," his father said.

The next day the Doctor and his two sons brought that trophy home, a symbol of his philosophy. "I've always tried to tell myself that the work itself is the thing, that win, lose, or draw, the work is really what counts," he once said. "As hard as it was to make myself believe that sometimes, it was the only thing I had to cling to each year—that every game, every night, I did the best I could."

Ewing and Olajuwon

Before the Doctor retired in 1987, two other players with that same work ethic loomed above the NBA horizon—Patrick Ewing and Hakeem Olajuwon, each a 7-foot center.

Tall at an early age, Ewing and Olajuwon each had been a soccer goaltender as a youngster in another land. Ewing grew up on the Caribbean island of Jamaica before moving with his family to Cambridge, Massachusetts, in 1975. Olajuwon lived in the sprawling African city of Lagos, Nigeria, before enrolling at the University of Houston.

Neither was a natural basketball player. "I knew," Ewing has said, "that it was something I'd have to work at." But by his tenth-grade season at Cambridge Rindge and Latin High School, he had worked at it hard enough to impress John Thompson, the Georgetown coach.

"With that kid," Thompson said, "we'll win the national championship."

With that kid, whose outstretched arms created a wingspan of nearly seven feet, Georgetown went to the Final Four three times in his four seasons. The Hoyas won the 1984 title, defeating Houston, with Olajuwon, 84–75. Twice the Hoyas were the runner-up, losing in 1982 to North Carolina, 63–62, on Michael Jordan's last-second shot, and in 1985 to Villanova, 66–64, in one of the NCAA tournament's most stunning upsets—not that it diminished Ewing's reputation.

"Patrick Ewing," said Rollie Masimino, the Villanova coach, "is the best player ever to play college basketball."

Two others, David Robinson and Shaquille O'Neal, each 7-1,

Patrick Ewing was a lottery bonanza for the Knicks.

soon arrived to challenge the dominance of Olajuwon and Ewing at center. Robinson, who missed two seasons while fulfilling his Navy service commitment, joined the San Antonio Spurs in 1990 and emerged as Rookie of the Year; four seasons later he won the scoring title with a 29.8 average. O'Neal, out of Louisiana State, joined

Shaquille O'Neal slam-dunks through friend and foe.

the Orlando Magic in 1992; two seasons later he led the NBA with a 29.3 average, but the Magic was swept in that year's NBA Finals by the Rockets.

"After the Finals were over," said the 301-pounder known as Shaq, "my father told me that I wasn't playing hard enough, and he was right."

O'Neal moved to the Lakers as a free agent in 1996, signing a seven-year, $120-million deal—an amount that didn't even include his size-22 sneaker contract and an occasional motion-picture appearance as an actor. But of the four centers, Hakeem Olajuwon emerged as the first to be on a championship team. When the Rockets won the NBA title in both 1994 and 1995, he justified his African name.

"Olajuwon," he once said. "It means being on top."

As a youngster in Lagos, where his father was a cement dealer, he was often bullied by other boys. "I had fights all the time. I was too tall, too thin," he explained. "They were picking on me because I was too abnormal." But as a teenager he played basketball on a Nigerian team coached by Chris Pond, a U.S. State Department worker. Pond arranged for Olajuwon to visit a few American colleges. On the list were Providence, Georgia Tech, and Oregon State, as well as the University of Houston.

"The day I arrived in New York, it was cold," Olajuwon once recalled. "I went on to Houston, where I was told it was warm."

At the time an American college education appealed more to Olajuwon and to his parents than the idea of playing basketball. But by his sophomore season at Houston, he was no longer too tall and too thin. Instead, he was too good for most other teams, just as Patrick Ewing was. In the 1984 NCAA title game, those two centers who had immigrated to America from other nations were the dominant centers on America's two best college teams—proof indeed that basketball had evolved into a world sport.

Through the years, basketball courts have been created almost everywhere—next to donkey trails in the hills of Greece; on snow-cleared areas in eastern Europe; in the dirt of India, where barefoot players were identified by numbers drawn in charcoal on their backs. Dr. James Naismith never realized what he started.

part **TWO**

**Kareem
Abdul-Jabbar,
a record
eighteen-time
All-Star,
displays his
sky hook.**

The Sky Hook and the Jumper

HE SCORED MORE POINTS THAN ANYBODY ELSE IN NBA history. He scored on all sorts of shots—dunks, tap-ins of rebounds, jumpers, short one-handers, finger-rolls, fadeaways, sometimes a creative shot dictated by the swarm of hands and arms around him. But when people think of Kareem Abdul-Jabbar, they think primarily of one shot. The sky hook. *His* sky hook.

"It's the ultimate shot," Pat Riley, his Los Angeles Laker coach, once said. "It's the greatest offensive weapon in sports."

Any weapon is only as effective as the person using it. And no other basketball player ever used the sky hook as effectively as Kareem, either right-handed or left-handed. Almost effortlessly the 7-2 center uncoiled out of the pivot, one knee rising, one hand holding the ball so high that when he shot, it appeared he was aiming down at the basket. Slowly the ball floated in a high arc, above and beyond the outstretched arms of any and all defenders, and swished through the net.

"It's what a lay-in is to anybody else," Magic Johnson says. "It's money."

More than anything else, it was Kareem Abdul-Jabbar's signature shot, discovered one day when he was nine years old. Then known as Lew Alcindor, he was already 5-8, by far the tallest kid in his fourth-grade class. He wasn't much of a player then. When he got into a game, his teammates seldom threw him the ball. But suddenly in a schoolyard game, a rebound fell to him near the right of the basket.

"With a guy from the other team at my back," he recalled in his autobiography, "I looked over my shoulder, saw the basket, turned into the lane, and with one hand put up my first hook shot. It missed, hit the back rim, and bounced out. But it felt right, and the next time I got the ball I tried it again. Neither of them went in, but I had found my shot."

He didn't know it at the time, but he also had found his career. Over his record twenty seasons with the Milwaukee Bucks and the Lakers, he had a record 38,387 points, an average of 24.6 a game. He was voted the Most Valuable Player Award a record six times. He was voted the Most Valuable Player in the championship finals twice, in 1971 and again in 1985, a tribute to the span of his skill, his stamina, and his shot.

"The perfection of that one shot has enabled him to endure," said Bob Lanier, a longtime rival center. "You know it's his favorite shot, but he never fails to hit it. It's the best hook I've seen. The perfect shot."

But like any shot, it had to be practiced—day after day, year after year. When the college rule makers abolished the dunk shot in 1967 (it later was reinstated), UCLA coach John Wooden realized that his All-America center must polish his hook shot. On his arrival from Power Memorial Academy in New York City, Kareem had what Wooden called a "flat" hook shot.

"I figured," Wooden has said, "he'd get better control if he turned his body more and snapped his wrist and fingers, while using his defender as a target to shoot over. We made him do it hundreds of times daily. It became a tremendous weapon."

As much as anything else, Kareem remembers how those practice sessions improved not merely the mechanics of his sky hook, but also his concentration while shooting it. In the sixth game of the 1974 championship playoff with the Celtics, his Milwaukee Bucks took a time-out with seven seconds remaining in the second overtime period and with the Celtics ahead, 101–100. When the Bucks were about to put the ball into play, he set a screen for Jon McGlocklin, but the Bucks' guard could not get open. Instead, the inbounds pass was thrown to Kareem near the foul line.

"I looked around and everyone was covered," he once recalled. "I felt as if everything was moving in slow motion and all power was mine. There was no sound. My head was clear. I don't think I've ever felt quite so totally, comfortably alone. I just dribbled to the baseline, turned, and put up the hook. It went right in."

That shot won the game, but the Celtics won the decisive seventh game. By then Kareem had established himself as a center who would be a ten-time All-NBA choice in an era that included such other prominent centers as Willis Reed, Dave Cowens, Bill Walton, and Moses Malone. He never played against Bill Russell, but during his first four seasons, he had to battle Wilt Chamberlain, still as strong as ever. Kareem, of course, was younger and quicker. He also developed a higher trajectory for his sky hook in order to thwart Wilt's height.

"I'd start right under the basket, then lean away a tiny bit, and put the ball at the top of the backboard," he once said. "Wilt would go after it every time, but it would go past his reach. I'd know from his body language he'd be thinking, 'That's not going in, it's up too high.' The ball would squeak against the top of the backboard above the rim and fall right through."

That's "touch," as coaches call it. Fingertip touch. One of the most important fundamentals for any shooter is releasing the ball from the fingertips, not from the palm of the hand, as Bill Russell discovered. For all his basketball ability as a rebounder and shot-blocker, Russell was never considered a good shooter. His explanation for that deficiency was rooted in his early years in Oakland, California, where he grew up. None of his early coaches taught him how to release the ball from his fingertips.

"I got into the habit of shooting with the palm of my hand instead," Russell has said. "I never really broke that bad habit."

Larry Bird's Confidence

Few, if any, shooters have had Larry Bird's fingertip touch, much less his concentration and confidence. When the NBA held its first Three-Point Shootout before the 1986 All-Star Game, Bird was one of eight entrants, along with Craig Hodges, Norm Nixon, Kyle Macy, Eric "Sleepy" Floyd, Trent Tucker, Leon Wood, and Dale Ellis. In their locker room before the contest, Bird stared at the others and smiled.

"Which one of you guys," he asked, "is going to finish second?"

Stunned, the other shooters tried to laugh off Bird's boast. But when the contest started, they quickly realized that the Celtics' forward was justifying the philosophy of Dizzy Dean, once an outspoken pitcher for the St. Louis Cardinals and later a TV announcer. "If you can back up what you say," Dean once said, "it ain't bragging."

Larry Bird shows his fingertip touch.

Bird backed it up. During the first shootaround from beyond the three-point line, Bird and Hodges emerged as the finalists. As they waited for the public-address announcer to introduce them, Bird turned to Hodges.

"Now I know," Bird said, "who's going to finish second."

In the final shootout, Bird dominated Hodges, 22–12, hitting 11 shots in a row. But for anyone who has seen Bird shoot, his triumph was not surprising. Like any great shooter, he practiced hours at a time, often by himself. After a team practice, he remained on the court alone with a basketball, as if he were a musician alone with his instrument. For the next hour, he did a solo like no other player. To get the feel of the ball, he dribbled it between his legs, then flung the ball against the gymnasium wall to simulate a pass, the ball returning to him as if it were on a rubber band attached to his right hand. Sweating now, he moved into his lay-up drill, ten shots with his right hand, ten with his left. He lofted his hook shot—from eight feet away, then ten, then twelve. He retreated to fire fifteen-foot jump shots, then he slid out beyond the three-point line. Almost all his shots swished through the net.

"Being out there alone, I've always liked it best that way," he once said. "At midnight when it's really quiet, or early in the morning when there's nobody else around."

He also liked it two hours before a game, when the Boston Garden's parquet floor was empty except for him. At first he shot free throws; then he fired three-point shots from the corners and from the perimeter beyond the foul circle, then a few fall-away jump shots.

"Everything is rhythm," he once said. "I'm not thinking about anything in the act of shooting—where my elbow is, any of that. Just rhythm."

For a foul-shooter, rhythm is even more important. He can take his time. He can shoot any way he wishes. Most players position themselves and shoot a one-hander, but the best foul-shooter in NBA history, Rick Barry, tossed his free throws underhanded. Bending his knees slightly, the 6-7 forward would twirl the ball from hip level. To some people, his style looked awkward. But the six-time All-NBA sharpshooter had a career 90 percent free-throw percentage.

"I just found it to be the most comfortable way to shoot free throws," Barry once said.

Away from the foul line, Barry hit jump shots with the best. He had an NBA career average of 23.2 points a game. When the Golden State Warriors won the 1975 title, he averaged 28.2 during the playoffs. On his jump shots, Barry was even more accurate than Bill Sharman, the sharpshooter of the early Celtics' championship teams who later coached the Lakers to the 1972 title. Sharman was a picture-perfect shooter.

"The elbow should be in close to the body," Sharman explained. "It shouldn't be in too tight or too far away. But it should definitely be close to the body and lined up with the basket so you have a good follow-through. And when you follow through, make sure you're going directly toward the basket."

"Mr. Clutch"

Sharman often used Jerry West's shooting form as an example. West, a ten-time All-NBA guard, is one of the few players selected for the All-Star Game every year throughout his career, which spanned fourteen seasons. His form surely contributed to his nickname of "Mr. Clutch," a tribute to his ability to score the winning basket in the final seconds even if surrounded by opposing defenders. In some of those clutch situations, West often drew an unintended foul.

"I've watched many players crowd Jerry when he goes up for that jump shot," Sharman said. "One of the reasons he's so hard to guard is because when he goes up for the shot, he has that elbow pointing toward the basket. So when the defender goes up to try to block Jerry's shot, he bumps Jerry's elbow and fouls him. Not only does keeping the elbow out in front make for a better shot, but it makes it that much tougher for anyone to guard you."

Like every great shooter, Jerry West was expected to shoot when he had the shot. But when Sam Jones joined the Celtics in 1957 out of little North Carolina Central College, he appeared to be in awe of his celebrated teammates.

In one of Jones's early games, he replaced Sharman alongside Bob Cousy in the Celtics' backcourt. Trying to get the rookie into the flow of the game, Cousy used a play that would set up Jones for a one-hander. But when the ball was passed to Jones, he hurriedly passed it back to Cousy, who found somebody else open. The next time down the court, Cousy set up another play for Jones, but again the rookie ignored the shot. Cousy turned toward Red Auerbach on the Celtic bench.

Unselfishly, Bob Cousy passed so others could shoot.

"Get him out of here," Cousy yelled. "If he won't shoot, put in somebody who will."

Hearing that, Jones understood that his more experienced teammates weren't about to complain if he shot the ball. Knowing he was a great shooter, they wanted him to shoot. And shoot Sam Jones did. He was on ten Celtic title-winning teams and averaged 25.9 points a game for the 1964 champions.

"I've never seen another player," his Celtic teammate Frank Ramsey once said, "who could get himself into a good shooting position as fast as Sam did."

Unlike most good shooters, who aim for the orange rim of the basket, Jones preferred to bank the ball off the glass backboard. But from the corner near the baseline, he had to shoot at the rim. Either way, when his career ended, he was the Celtics' second-leading career scorer, behind Cousy. In six seasons he led the Celtics in field-goal percentage during an era when Bill Russell was taking much shorter shots. By the time Jones departed after the 1969 playoffs, John Havlicek was established as a Celtic sharpshooter.

"I wasn't a shooter the way Sam was," Havlicek said. "I didn't have Sam's touch. I learned to score by taking advantage of every opening."

Havlicek created that opening by running and running until it developed. "The toughest guy for me to score on," he once explained, "was the guy who kept after me all the time—nose to nose, basket to basket. And the opposite is also true. The toughest guy to defend against is the guy who keeps running, who never lets up, who never lets you relax." At 6-5, he could play either forward or guard. He followed Frank Ramsey as the Celtics' "sixth man," meaning the player who came off the bench after the game has started, but Havlicek usually played more minutes than most of the starters.

"It doesn't matter who starts," Red Auerbach often said. "It's who finishes."

With a game on the line at the finish, Havlicek displayed the essence of every great shooter—wanting to take the shot that determined whether his team would win or lose in the last few seconds.

"I want the ball in a tight situation," he once said. "I'm not bothered if I miss. As long as you know it's the best you could have done, you should not second-guess a shot."

Pistol Pete's Explosion

Pete Maravich never second-guessed a shot. The 6-5 guard known as "Pistol Pete" averaged 28 shots a game for the New Orleans Jazz during the 1976–77 season, but he also averaged 31.1 points that season, including 68 in a game against the Knicks. During his NBA career, he averaged 24.2 points a game. He was a shooter who never thought he would miss. As a three-time All-America at Louisiana State, where his father, Press Maravich,

Hair and socks flopping, Pete Maravich never thought he'd miss.

was the coach, Pete's career average of 44.2 points a game is the highest in NCAA history. He scored 69 points against Alabama and 66 against Tulane. In the second half of a game against St. John's, he scored 41. He had floppy hair and wore floppy socks. He could spin the ball on his fingers and bounce it off his head. But above all, he was a shooter.

"My game is still explosion," he said after having a 30-point game with the Jazz. "I knew there was no reason to hold back. I could've shot from forty feet, and it would've gone in because I had my game going."

But for all of Pistol Pete's points, he never quite attained the stature of another LSU product, Bob Pettit, a 6-9 forward with the St. Louis Hawks who was a member of the All-NBA team for ten consecutive seasons. Taller than most forwards at the time, Pettit was a two-time winner of the Most Valuable Player Award, in 1956 and again in 1959, the same seasons that he led the NBA in scoring. During his career, he averaged 26.4 points a game.

"Bob was great," Cousy once said, "because he understood his limitations. He would be out there fifteen feet away, and he would take one dribble and shoot. He knew one dribble was it."

Pettit scored 50 points in a 1958 playoff game against the Celtics, tying the NBA playoff record that Cousy had set in a four-overtime victory over the Syracuse Nats in 1953 when the Celtic playmaker sank 30 of 32 foul shots. Four years later Elgin Baylor scored 61 against the Celtics in the championship series, establishing the play-off record that endured until Michael Jordan of the Chicago Bulls produced 63 against the Celtics in 1986 after having scored 49 in the first game of their opening-round series. Jumping high to shoot one-handers and soaring to the basket for his flying dunks, the 6-5 Jordan scored a total of 112 points in two games in the Boston Garden against that year's NBA champions.

"I've never had my vertical leap measured," Jordan has said, "but sometimes I think about how high I get up. I always spread my legs when I jump high, and it seems like I've opened a parachute that slowly brings me back to the floor."

Jordan was voted the NBA's Rookie of the Year in 1985 while averaging 28.2 points a game. But early in his second season he suffered a broken foot. Hoping to prevent the possibility of his reinjuring the foot, the Bulls preferred that he not return until the following season. But a month before the playoffs began, he insisted on playing. In the playoffs he was as dazzling as ever, if not even better.

"He's a cross between Jerry West and a younger Julius Erving," Mike Thibault, a Bulls assistant coach, once said. "He has West's jump shot and outside scoring ability and the Doc's scoring ability going to the basket."

Michael Jordan's Trampoline

Kareem Abdul-Jabbar had his sky hook, and Larry Bird was deadly from behind the three-point line or on a driving lay-up. Michael Jordan can hit a quick jumper from anywhere, but his artistry as a shooter is based on improvisation. Jordan also developed another dimension somewhat similar to that of Earl "The Pearl" Monroe, a whirling dervish for the Baltimore Bullets and later for the 1973 champion Knicks.

"Michael does what Earl 'The Pearl' used to do," said Jerry Krause,

Tongue out, Michael Jordan slams.

the Bulls' general manager, "only he does it three feet higher."

Three feet higher, Jordan seemed to be playing basketball on a trampoline, floating up there in the Air that was his sneakers' trademark.

"Elevating, he can shoot or pass from there," says Hubie Brown, the television analyst who coached the Atlanta Hawks and the Knicks, "but let's add another thing. On the way up, at the final moment, if two big men fly at him, he can arch back at some new angle and still get off a shot. Or he turns his shoulders and slithers through, like his body has disappeared, and comes out the other side. Many men can do the two things, pass to the free man or get off a shot, but they don't have three options like Michael does."

No matter how or where he shoots, his accuracy is almost uncanny.

"Every time it leaves his hand," Brown says, "you think it's going in."

While winning a record nine NBA scoring titles, Jordan has averaged 31.7 points a game over his career, the highest in NBA history—higher than Wilt Chamberlain's 30.1, Elgin Baylor's 27.4, and Jerry West's 27.0. And he has accomplished it by creating shots that other players never dream of.

"Many, many times I've been on that high," he once said. "Those are times when I do things that other people can't do and wish they could. My intention always is to score, but with that creativity—the dunking, the creativity of it, the fun."

It's fun for him, but it's never fun for the players assigned to defend him. They worry that they will be frozen forever on a "poster" shot, a Jordan move that will be photographed and reproduced on a poster with his defender appearing helpless, wondering where he went and what happened. Even the NBA's best defenders, like Joe Dumars of the Detroit Pistons, always worried.

"He once dropped 63 on me," Dumars said. "He had his jumper going. He wasn't even looking to drive—63, and he didn't drive more than five or six times."

Jordan even amazed himself occasionally with a move that not

Michael Jordan rises to the occasion in the 1993 NBA finals.

only fooled his defender but that he had never done before or even tried in practice.

"Sometimes I'll see a move and I'll say, 'How'd I do that?'" he has said. "You can't explain it, yet you do it. It's instinct, just happens. You don't really think about it, and you can't work it. You've just got to have it."

No other basketball player has had it like Michael Jordan.

When Small Is Tall

NOT LONG AFTER JOHN STOCKTON, A VIRTUALLY UNKNOWN point guard at Gonzaga University, had been chosen by the Utah Jazz with the sixteenth choice in the first round of the 1984 NBA draft, Jazz broadcaster Hot Rod Hundley phoned him. In the background Stockton could hear noise.

"Are they booing?" Stockton asked.

"They're not saying, 'Boo,'" Hundley said. "They're saying, 'Who?'"

Nobody is asking, "Who?" now. With over 12,000 career assists entering the 1997–98 season, John Stockton held the NBA record. As a pure passer and playmaker, the Jazz's point guard, a member of the Olympic Dream Team in both 1992 and 1996, has been hailed as equal, if not superior, to any of the old-timers, even Bob Cousy, the Boston Celtics' magician in the NBA's early years.

"John," said Magic Johnson, "is by far the best floor leader there

John Stockton's sleight of hand hypnotizes defenders.

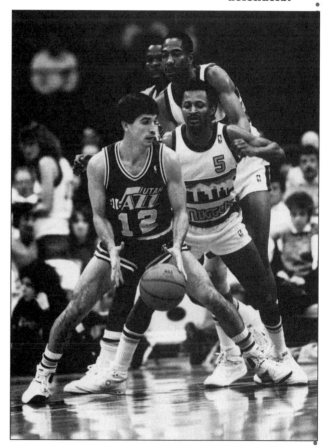

is, in terms of leading his team and making the pass and getting everybody where they should be in the offense. His whole thing is to get everybody involved."

Growing up in Spokane, Washington, only a few blocks from Gonzaga Prep and Gonzaga University, he was the little brother who tagged along with his older brother Steve to the nearby playgrounds and gyms. But he soon learned how to persuade the other teenagers to let him play.

"I fed them the ball," he recalled with a grin.

At every level of basketball—high school, college, or NBA—Stockton kept feeding his teammates the ball, the test for a true point guard who thinks first about setting up his teammates rather than scoring himself. And he did it without trying to be fancy. Nobody appreciated that more than Karl Malone, the longtime Jazz power forward who also was a two-time Dream Team member.

"John doesn't go behind his back or cross-over dribble," Malone said. "I've never seen him go between his legs. He's not show. He gets you the ball at the right time. He's the smartest player I've ever seen."

Inch for inch and pound for pound, Stockton is also one of the NBA's toughest players. Some small guards are reluctant to set screens for their teammates, especially in the NBA, with so many huge bodies banging around. Stockton never flinches, never jumps out of a screen after setting it so he might be in position to shoot himself.

"I've been asked if I enjoy passing or scoring more," he said, "but depending on the point in the game and what's necessary, if you can deliver the play that helps win the game, whatever that is, that's what I enjoy. If it's a screen and you get a guy open and he scores a big basket, that gives me as much of a charge as anything."

Small size never deterred Stockton or Tyrone "Muggsy" Bogues, a 5-3 point guard for the Charlotte Hornets.

"I never looked at myself as being small," Bogues often said. "I just look at myself as a basketball player."

Tyrone "Muggsy" Bogues plays much bigger than his 5-3 height.

"All Different Packages"

That philosophy has stirred all the outstanding small players in NBA history. Slater Martin, at 5-10 and 175, was the playmaker on the Minneapolis Lakers' five championship teams and also on the

For Isiah Thomas, "that rhythm, that flow" was like no other feeling.

St. Louis Hawks' 1958 championship team. One of the NBA's best little big men was Calvin Murphy, at 5-9 and 165 pounds. Over his thirteen seasons with the Houston Rockets, he averaged 17.9 points a game, with a high of 25.8 points a game in 1978, and his streak of 78 consecutive free throws set an NBA record.

Isiah Thomas, the point guard on the 1989 and 1990 champion Detroit Pistons and later a vice-president of the Toronto Raptors, also was smaller than most of his teammates in the Chicago playgrounds.

"But when I was a kid," Thomas said, "I never let size become an issue. The main thing is developing your skills and using the talent that God has given you. Good players come in all different packages. I went to work, and the longer I was involved, the more fun it became for me. I get real joy from the sport; I just love it. And it's that enthusiasm that makes me drive myself to become the best player I can possibly be."

In the 1984 All-Star Game, Thomas indeed was the best player, with 21 points, 15 assists, 5 rebounds, and 4 steals.

"That was a great thrill," he said, "because it meant that for one day I was considered the best basketball player in the world."

Although not that tall at 6-1, the playmaker on Indiana's 1981

NCAA championship team emerged as a shooter who averaged more than 20 points a game for the Pistons while setting an NBA season record in 1985 with an average of 13.9 assists a game. During the final minutes of an important game, he took charge as few other players do. In the 1984 playoffs against the Knicks, he scored 16 points in a span of only 94 seconds.

"You just get into the rhythm," he explained. "And when you get into that rhythm, that flow, it's like no other feeling you can describe. It's just there."

Thomas has been described as the NBA's purest point guard—a scorer when the shot is there, but primarily a passer and playmaker who controls his team's offense. In previous years, the Pistons had another point guard, Kevin Porter, who held the NBA season assist record until Thomas broke it. Like all great passers, Porter understood that a pass has to be thrown to the right player in the right spot at the right time.

"I knew I could throw it up to the rim and Terry Tyler would dunk it," Porter once said. "I knew M. L. Carr liked it out on the wing and Bob Lanier loved that little turnaround jumper in the post. John Long had that little set shot."

"Aware of Everybody"

Through his first seven Laker seasons, Magic Johnson had the highest assist average in NBA history—10.7 a game. "When he's in control," K. C. Jones, the Celtic coach, said, "there's no one like him." But even among point guards, Magic has a gift that few others possess. "Magic is aware of everybody," said Bill Bertka, a Laker assistant coach. "During a game, most guards know how the other guards are playing, and the big men can keep track of all the other big men, but Magic can come into a time-out and know who's doing what. He knows who's turning his head on defense, who's dogging it, and who's playing hard. Magic sees everything, and he understands everything he sees." As a point guard should.

Maurice Cheeks, the 76er "coach on the floor"

Maurice Cheeks's passes set up Julius Erving and Moses Malone when the 76ers won the 1983 NBA championship with Billy Cunningham as their coach.

"When the 76ers went into any series or any individual game," said Dave Wohl, later the New Jersey Nets' coach but then a Laker assistant coach, "Billy Cunningham knew that with Maurice in charge, he never had anything to worry about. He will get very few turnovers. He will get open-floor scoring. He knows the ball will get to the right man. And he knows the tempo will always be whatever he wants. He was the extension of Billy's thought on the floor. It's like computer language."

At first, that "computer language" was often their only means of communication. As a rookie, Cheeks didn't say much.

"It takes a while for me to know people around me," Cheeks said. "Once I get to know them, I'm a lot more vocal."

Cheeks had been hoping to be chosen by his hometown Chicago Bulls in the 1978 draft. When the 76ers took him in the second round, his father, Moses, walked to the front of the hotel ballroom where executives of other NBA teams were sitting at small tables.

"You'll be sorry you didn't draft my son," his father scolded. "You'll be sorry."

Passers and playmakers often are ignored in the draft. General managers and coaches look for 7-footers, for shooters, for strong rebounders. If a passer and playmaker is also a good shooter, he is likely to be chosen early in the first round, as Magic Johnson and Isiah Thomas were. But unless he's looked upon as a potential scorer, the passer and playmaker usually is drafted as an afterthought, as Paul Pressey of the Milwaukee Bucks was. But when Don Nelson realized that Pressey was special, the Bucks' coach invented a new position—point forward.

"Even though Press is a forward," Nelson explained, "we often let him bring the ball up the way a point guard would."

Pressey's presence in the backcourt forced the opposing team to realign its defense. To cover the 6-5 Pressey, a forward had to pick him up in an unfamiliar area. And with Pressey dribbling the ball upcourt, it eased the burden on the Bucks' guards and enabled Nelson to use two guards who would prefer not to be responsible for bringing the ball upcourt.

"Playing point forward," Pressey said, "gives me a chance to emphasize the strongest part of my game—passing."

As with just about everything else in basketball, passing and play-making has been a Boston Celtics' tradition. On their way to the 1986 NBA championship, the Celtics seemed to be almost passing the ball too much. "Sometimes the ball is moving so much," Dennis Johnson said, "we're passing up as many as three or four shots." But inevitably all those passes usually create an easy shot.

"There is no player," Kevin McHale said of the Celtics' philosophy, "who can outrun a ball that is passed."

Executing the Fast Break

On most teams the best passer is usually the playmaker. But on the Celtics the best passer was Larry Bird, the high-scoring 6-9 forward with the instincts of a point guard. "My high school coach told me," Bird said, "that a pass is no good unless the player you pass the ball to can receive it in shooting position. If I'm making a bounce pass, I try to get the ball to bounce up real smooth, so that the player can go right into the flow of his shot." On the fast break, Bird tried to get the ball to his teammate just as his teammate was swooping toward the basket. Ever since Bob Cousy was the Celtics' playmaker, their fast break has been one of their primary weapons.

"Cousy," said Red Auerbach, his Celtic coach, "just happened to be the best guard who ever lived when it came to the execution of the fast break."

For a fast break to develop before the opposing team gets back on defense, perhaps the most important pass is what is known as the outlet—the pass to the guard near midcourt from the rebounder who has grabbed the opposing team's missed shot.

A fast break develops when the playmaker looks downcourt the moment he catches the outlet pass from the rebounder.

"When you get the ball," Auerbach said, "the first thing you do is look before you pass. This is very important. It doesn't slow you up that much. You're only talking about a fraction of a second. If you just throw by instinct, there's a good chance the other team will pick off your pass. Ideally you start the break down the side where the rebound came. But if you look first and maybe spot a teammate breaking into the open, that's got to be the best two points in the world. If you don't look, you don't see him. The break is no good if he has to yell, 'Hey, hey, hey.'"

Although the best passers are usually smaller guards and forwards, the outlet pass is usually thrown by a center. Over a decade after Wes Unseld stopped playing for the Washington Bullets, he is still considered to have been the best outlet passer. At 6-7 and a burly 245 pounds, he would go up, grab the rebound, then turn and fire the ball to midcourt while still in midair.

"There was nobody like Wes," said Kevin Loughery, later the Bullets' coach, but then one of their guards. "And if you weren't looking for that pass, it would take your head off."

Once the guard has the ball on the fast break, he dribbles upcourt, searching for an open teammate. To do that, the guard can't be looking at the ball as he dribbles. Instead, he dribbles by feel, knowing where the ball is and where it will be in the next split second. To do that without thinking, a youngster needs to learn to dribble without looking at the ball.

"It's not that hard," Pete Maravich said. "Bounce the ball behind you, to the side, and in front of you. Then get on your knees and bounce it in a circle around your body and between your legs. But never look at the ball. After a while, you'll find it's easy."

If a fast break doesn't develop, the playmaker must slow his dribble and set up whatever play the coach wants at that time. For that play to produce a basket, ideally it will create an open man, a shooter who will be momentarily uncovered by a defensive player. When the Knicks were winning the 1970 and 1973 NBA championships, their coach, Red Holzman, would remind his players over and over about that.

"Hit the open man," Holzman would say.

In order for a shooter to get open, he must learn to move without the ball, as Bill Bradley did so effectively on those championship Knick teams. Later a United States senator from New Jersey, Bradley had been a Rhodes Scholar at Princeton as well as an All-America basketball player. Not as fast as some players and not much of a jumper, Bradley learned how to move without the ball in order to get open for his short one-handers.

"Young players," Bradley said,

Bill Bradley, a Rhodes Scholar and a United States senator

"have a tendency to neglect moving without the ball, but it's one of the most important phases of the game. When you pass the ball, you have to make sure you move immediately after the ball is passed and always move away, not toward, the player to whom you've passed."

As those Knicks proved then, and as all the best NBA teams continue to prove, you move without the ball in order to get open and take a pass to shoot the ball. But as important as good shooters are, every good shooter needs players who are willing to pass the ball.

Hard Work

WITH HIS GRACEFUL TURNAROUND JUMP SHOT, HAKEEM Olajuwon is one of the NBA's most spectacular scorers. At 7 feet, he is also known for his rebounding. In leading the Houston Rockets to consecutive championships in 1994 and 1995, he made people appreciate him not only as a man-to-man defensive player covering other centers but as a shot-blocker.

"Hakeem is the best center ever," said Clyde Drexler, his Rockets teammate, who also was his teammate a decade earlier at the University of Houston. "The NBA has had many great centers, but how many of them have Hakeem's skills at both ends of the floor? How many of them do it every game? He's the only one."

In basketball's archives Hakeem Olajuwon will be remembered not so much for his points and his rebounds as for his blocked shots. With his final block of the 1995–96 season, he established an NBA career record of 3,190, one more than Kareem Abdul-Jabbar's total. But the Rockets' center needed only twelve seasons to accomplish what took the Hall of Fame center twenty.

Olajuwon's work ethic, developed in his Nigerian upbringing, has separated him from most players.

"I'm still learning the game," he often says. "I'll be learning the game until I retire. And when I retire, I'll say, 'I should've done this.'"

That philosophy is typical of why he has developed into a dominant two-way player in a relatively short time.

"One of my pet peeves," said Les Alexander, the Rockets' owner during their two championship seasons, "is that some players don't work on their game. Some guys are the same player five years later,

Hakeem Olajuwon putting one through for the Rockets

but Hakeem never stops working. Sometimes when you watch him on the court, you'll catch him smiling. He just seems so happy."

As a youngster in Lagos, Nigeria, in central Africa, Olajuwon didn't play basketball until he was fifteen, much later than most Americans. Growing up tall, the third of six children in a middle-class family, he played soccer and team handball.

"I was taller than all the other kids because Nigerians on the average are short," he recalled. "I always stood out in the crowd. I was criticized, and people made fun of me. I wasn't comfortable. I felt I was too tall. My father was concerned. Most of the tall guys ended up bent over because they didn't want to stand straight. They tried to hide. They were not proud they were tall. That's one thing my family made me understand. Be proud. Stand tall. I started believing it."

Around that time Oliver Johnson, an American stationed with the Peace Corps in Lagos, noticed this tall teenage soccer goaltender with quick feet.

"I was his special project," Olajuwon said. "He tried to get me to play basketball for a long time. I finally agreed to try it. I played once and fell in love with the game. At first I was just reckless, playing on raw talent. I just played, wasting energy. Now I do more things."

When he arrived at the University of Houston in 1980, he was still a raw talent, but he soon polished that talent.

"Basketball is a team game," he said. "The goal is to win the championship. That's the team goal. That is my goal."

The Ultimate Defensive Weapon

The blocked shot is the ultimate weapon in basketball defense. It's also a psychological weapon, as Bill Russell proved during the Celtics' streak of NBA championships.

"Blocking a shot is worse than dunking on a guy," Russell said. "When you dunk on a guy, it tells him something. But it usually only gets him mad. Blocking a guy's shot scares him. He may challenge you once, twice, or even three times. But if you just get to block a couple of his shots, you'll have him thinking about where you are every time he gets ready to shoot."

Most shot-blockers are what Red Auerbach, the coach of nine championship Celtic teams, called "shot-swatters," meaning those who block shots any way they can, swatting the ball out of bounds or perhaps into the hands of another opposing shooter. Only a few play-ers have been able to block shots with a purpose, as Russell did.

Patrick Ewing reaches to block a shot.

"Russell made shot-blocking an art," Auerbach said. "He would pop the ball straight up and grab it like a rebound, or else redirect it into the hands of one of his teammates, and we'd be off and running on the fast break. You never saw Russell bat a ball into the third balcony the way those other guys did."

As soon as Russell joined the Celtics in 1956, they developed a reputation for defense that coin-cided with their NBA domina-tion for more than a decade. Basketball teams win champi-onships more with defense than with offense. Many teams know how to score, but not every team knows how to stop the other team from scoring. This isn't to say that defense is based on secret strategy.

"Defense means hard work,"

Red Auerbach often said. "You play defense until you get the ball. Your defensive responsibilities are not complete until you get the ball."

Through the years the Celtics have had several of the NBA's most respected defensive players, especially Russell, the 6-9 center with the long arms. His teammates always knew that Russell was back there behind them, ready to help out if an opposing player drove to the basket. In those years the Celtics had what their players called a "Hey, Bill" defense.

"We always knew," Bob Cousy said, "that if somebody got by us, we could yell, 'Hey, Bill,' and Bill would pick him up."

Russell's willingness to work on defense rubbed off on his teammates. If he was willing to work, to hustle, to dive for a loose ball, they had to work, to hustle, to dive for a loose ball. But by nature, some of Russell's teammates were outstanding defensive players, notably K. C. Jones, then a smooth guard who had developed his defensive instincts while playing with Russell at the University of San Francisco.

"K.C. was probably the best defensive guard who ever played," his Celtic teammate Bill Sharman said. "I remember one night when K.C. was guarding a man who was having a tremendous night. K.C. finally put his hands down at his sides and started stamping his feet. The player was so startled, he threw the ball away. Another time, I saw K.C. start waving his arms frantically at the man he was guarding. Anything to distract him."

"Havlicek Stole the Ball!"

Just as John Havlicek never seemed to stop running on offense, he never stopped hounding his man on defense. No matter what the situation, he never surrendered.

Havlicek's moment on defense occurred in the 1965 playoffs. In the decisive seventh game of the Eastern Division final, the Celtics were leading the 76ers, 110–109, with five seconds to play. But the 76ers were about to take the ball out of bounds under the Celtics' basket. With a quick score, the 76ers would dethrone the Celtics, who had won six consecutive NBA championships. Near the basket, Russell was leaning against Wilt Chamberlain, trying to keep his 7-foot rival from positioning himself for Hal Greer's inbounds pass. While the two centers grappled, Greer tossed a lob pass to Chet Walker, a 6-6 forward who would have three options. He could pass to Wilt, or pass back to Greer, or drive himself. But as Walker waited for the lob pass to come down, the voice of Johnny Most, the Celtics' radio announcer, burst into homes and autos everywhere in New England.

"Havlicek stole the ball!" Most screamed. "Havlicek stole the ball! Havlicek stole the ball!"

Havlicek had leaped and deflected the ball to Sam Jones, who dribbled upcourt, killing the final seconds. Havlicek's steal had kept the Celtics on their throne.

Another worker on defense was Jerry West, the Lakers guard (and later their Executive Vice-President of Basketball Operations). Although best known as "Mr. Clutch" for his shooting skill in the final minutes, West was a three-time member of the NBA's all-defensive team. Like most good defensive players, he had what coaches like to call a "nose for the ball." But every so often his nose got in the way. He suffered a broken nose nine times.

"My wife," West often joked, "has been married to nine different guys. Every time my nose gets broken, I look different."

Another all-defensive team selection was Walt Frazier, the quick-handed guard of the Knicks' 1970 and 1973 championship teams. Frazier's hands were so quick, he could snatch a fly out of the air. In recent years the Knicks' defense revolved around Patrick Ewing, their 7-foot center who reminds old-timers of Bill Russell, not only on defense but also in his desire to win. John Thompson, who coached Ewing at Georgetown nearly two decades after having been a backup center to Russell on the Celtics, has seen them both.

"They share an amazingly similar level of sensitivity," Thompson

Walt Frazier showing his touch in an All-Star game

has said. "That's the biggest thing, their pride and their will to win. A lot of people have the will to *play*, but few have the will to *win*. Patrick didn't think we could look good if we were losing. Neither did Russ."

Neither do most of the NBA's best defensive players. Michael Cooper of the Lakers developed that attitude as a youngster. While playing in a Pasadena, California, backyard with his uncle's puppies, he slipped. His left leg landed on the jagged edge of a coffee can. He needed one hundred stitches to close the wounds. Inside the leg, muscles and ligaments were damaged. Doctors warned him that he might never walk properly again.

"I was six years old, and I had to wear a knee brace after that," Cooper said. "The other kids would be out playing, but I could only watch. One day when I was thirteen, I just took off the brace. I couldn't stand it anymore. And wherever I went, I ran—to the store, on the sidewalks, even out to get the paper in the morning. And it's like I've been running ever since. Especially in basketball."

In the 1980 championship series, the 6-7 forward was assigned to cover Julius Erving of the 76ers.

"Doctor J is a legend to me," Cooper said. "I've watched him on television since I was a little kid. He's my idol."

In the opener, Cooper controlled his idol, limiting Doctor J to 24 points as the Lakers won, 109–102, on their way to the NBA title, four games to two.

"I woke up at four-fifteen this morning," Cooper said later. "I just sat up in bed. The game was jammin' through my mind. I was nervous until I got on the court."

Out on the court, a good defensive player does things that never appear in the standard NBA box score, which is geared mostly to offensive statistics. Defensive rebounds, blocked shots, and steals are listed, but a defensive player's value often depends on more subtle maneuvers. Taking a charge, for example. Holding your position against a player driving to the basket, hoping that an offensive "charging" foul will be whistled. But almost every time, the defensive player will be sent sprawling to the court.

"They should come up with a statistic for taking the charge," Cooper suggested. "It takes a lot of guts to step in front of Moses Malone or Charles Barkley. You also should have a stat for floor burns."

Bobby Jones and DJ

But for Bobby Jones, the standard box score always told enough. At least certain categories did. As a 6-9 forward with the 76ers and the

Nuggets for twelve seasons, Jones was considered one of the NBA's most tireless players. Asked once to describe his ideal box-score line, he never hesitated.

"Five offensive rebounds," he said. "Five defensive rebounds, ten assists, five blocked shots, five steals, and no turnovers in twenty-five minutes."

Jones, typically, never mentioned points. Over his career, he had a dependable scoring average of 12 points a game, in both the regular season and the playoffs. He was on the 76ers' 1983 championship team. He appeared in four All-Star games. But his 76ers' coach, Billy Cunningham, once said, "Bobby Jones *is* defense." And he will be remembered for defense.

"In high school in Charlotte, my feet were bigger than anyone else's, so I played defense because I was so uncoordinated," he once explained. "And at North Carolina, I didn't have that many points. I just learned to move the ball, play hard defense, help out on defense. For me that was just my game."

Another dominating defensive player was Dennis Johnson, known as "DJ," the Celtics' guard on their 1984 and 1986 championship teams. Before the Celtics acquired him from the Phoenix Suns, he had been a defensive factor when the Seattle SuperSonics won the 1979 title. Even though Johnson covered opposing guards, his efficiency was obvious to players at other positions.

"People always say you make things happen on offense," Lakers' forward Michael Cooper said, "but DJ makes things happen on defense."

In obtaining Johnson in 1983, the Celtics were hoping he would make things happen primarily in the playoffs. At the time Red Auerbach, the Celtics' president, was still steaming from the memory of the Celtics having been swept out of the Eastern Conference playoffs by the Milwaukee Bucks in four games. In the Eastern Conference final the year before, the Celtics had been eliminated by the 76ers in seven games. In each series, the Celtics had been unable to control two outside shooters—Sidney Moncrief of the Bucks and Andrew Toney of the 76ers.

"Now that you're here," K. C. Jones, the Celtics' coach, told Johnson in training camp, "we can win a championship."

On their way to that 1984 championship, the Celtics eliminated the Bucks in five games. On their way to the 1986 title, the Celtics swept the Bucks in four games. Before losing the 1985 championship series to the Lakers, the Celtics eliminated the 76ers in seven games. In each of those series, the freckle-faced 6-4 guard known as "DJ" controlled either Moncrief or Toney, not that he shut them down completely.

"What I consider a great defensive job is when DJ doesn't let somebody score a lot of baskets in a row," K. C. Jones said. "DJ doesn't let anybody get hot. Anytime that DJ is guarding a guy, that guy knows it. Instead of worrying about scoring, that guy is worrying about DJ. They keep thinking, DJ is on me, DJ is on me. You name a player, and DJ is a force against them."

Quick Hands

Sidney Moncrief was a force on defense as well as offense. Like all good defensive players, he described what he did as mostly hard work, hounding his opponent.

"But it's also technique and dedication," the supple 6-4 guard added. "It doesn't take a whole lot of natural ability. I think everyone has the potential to be a good defensive player. But if your coaches before you get to the NBA don't emphasize it, the chances of a player feeling the obligation to play good defense isn't there. In the NBA, defense utilizes the team concept, at least for the good teams. The players are so good offensively, you have to play the percentages and gamble occasionally. The type of players behind you make a big difference."

Moncrief learned his work ethic as a youngster in Little Rock, Arkansas, where his mother toiled as a hotel maid.

"Before she left every morning she handed me a list of chores that I had to get done before she came home," he recalled. "The threat of punishment was all we needed to keep us in line. Even when she wasn't around, we knew there were certain things we had to do and certain ways we had to act. It gave me a very strong foundation to work from. Everything you do at home carries over into what you do in life. And for me it did carry over onto the basketball court. I was hesitant about doing anything halfway."

In analyzing opponents, Moncrief had a plan in covering the NBA's best shooters—Magic Johnson, for example.

"Take away his right," Moncrief once said. "Don't let him shoot a set shot; make him move when he shoots."

Magic was a concern to every guard assigned to cover him, even Alvin Robertson, who set an NBA record in 1986 with 301 steals for the San Antonio Spurs.

"You've got to get Magic in the backcourt," Robertson said. "Don't let him get a full head of steam."

With his quick hands, Robertson was a concern to the guards he covered. After a basket, he would appear about to drift upcourt, but suddenly he would snatch the other team's lazy inbounds pass and score an easy basket.

"He's a pest," said Rolando Blackman of the Dallas Mavericks. "He can disrupt your offense. He's constantly in motion."

But in the NBA, the quick hands of a pest are never as intimidating on defense as the big hands of a shot-blocker. One of the most intimidating shot-blockers of recent years was Mark Eaton, a husky 7-4 center who was listed at 290 pounds.

"Shooting over him," said Mychal Thompson, then with the Portland Trail Blazers, "is like shooting over the Great Wall of China."

Despite his size, Eaton might have never played in the NBA were it not for Tom Lubin, an assistant coach at Cypress (California) Junior College, who spotted him working in a tire store. Although nearly seven feet tall when he was graduated from Westminster (California)

High School, Eaton had no offers to play college basketball. He attended a trade school in Arizona, then went to work in the tire store where Lubin found him.

"It took Tom about two months to convince me to try playing basketball," Eaton said. "I'd been away from it for three years."

After two seasons at Cypress, he enrolled at UCLA and played there for two seasons. He was hardly a star. On the last road trip of his final season, he was left behind. Even so, the Jazz drafted him on the fourth round.

"We took him," said Frank Layden, the longtime Jazz coach, "because you can't coach height."

You can coach basketball theft, the knack of knowing how to steal the ball as adeptly as another Jazz player, John Stockton, does. But in setting the NBA record for career steals with over 2,500 entering the 1997–98 season, even Stockton needed time to learn the tricks of the trade.

"John used to be out there chasing guys around," said Jerry Sloan, the Jazz coach, "but he learned that you rarely pick off someone in the open court. You get your steals by using your hands in traffic, by doubling down on the big men, or by playing the passing lanes."

It's all defense, the part of the game that often wins the game.

REBOUNDING

Position and Timing

OF ALL THE SKILLS IN BASKETBALL, REBOUNDING DEMANDS the most devotion, the most energy. It is work, not play. You play basketball, but you work at rebounding. The only fun is when you get the rebound, especially if you get more rebounds than anybody else. Even then it's because you've worked at it.

For all the different colors he dyes his hair, for all his outrageous incidents, Dennis Rodman works at rebounding.

"There's more to it than being able to jump higher than the next guy," he has said. "A lot of the work is done before you even jump. I know shooters, but that's not enough. You have to watch the flight of the ball. Most guys see the shot go up; then they turn and look at the rim, waiting for the ball to come off. I watch the ball in the air and make an adjustment if I need to."

At 6-8, Rodman is not as tall as many of his opponents, but at a lean, muscular 215 pounds, he has the timing and the tricks. He also studies the shot trajectories of his teammates and opponents.

"Anytime I see Michael Jordan or Scottie Pippen shoot from the top of the key," he said, "I know the ball will come off the rim to the right. Other guys, if they have a high arc on their shot, that usually means the ball will bounce high off the rim."

As the tattooed power forward who helped the Bulls win the 1996 NBA title with a playoff average of 13.7 rebounds a game and a season average of 14.9, he created a cult.

"I rebound with a little flair, a little something extra," he said with a smile. "It's not for the crowd. It's just for me. Rebounding is how I express myself on the floor."

Although Rodman did not play basketball in high school, he expressed himself so well at Southeastern Oklahoma State that the Pistons chose him in the second round of the 1986 draft. His rebounds helped the Pistons win the NBA title in 1989 and again in 1990.

"Most guys are straight-up jumpers," said Johnny "Red" Kerr, the Bulls' broadcaster who played for the Syracuse Nats against Wilt Chamberlain and Bill Russell, "but Dennis can adjust his body in the air. The only other player I've seen who could do that was Russell."

Upon joining the Celtics from the 1956 Olympic team, Russell explained rebounding to Coach Red Auerbach as no one ever had.

"You know, Red," said Russell, "everything in rebounding is timing and position, because eighty percent of all rebounds are taken below the rim."

Bill Russell grabs one of his 21,620 regular-season rebounds.

In recalling that conversation later, Auerbach mentioned, "It showed me how Russ thought about the game. He had reduced rebounding to a science. His rebounds were not accidents. He knew exactly what he was doing. Every time the ball went up in the air, Russell rebounded or boxed out or did something. He was never a spectator. If he found himself out of a play, the very least he would do was box out. But usually he'd release his man and move in to dominate the boards." Ever since Russell dominated the boards as no other player ever has, rebounders have described what they do by reciting Russell's credo—position and timing.

The NBA season record average of 27.2 rebounds was set by Wilt Chamberlain in 1961 with his record 2,149 rebounds. In a game against Russell and the Celtics that season, Wilt had 55 rebounds, another record. NBA players have grabbed 40 or more rebounds in a game twenty-four times. Wilt did it fourteen of those times, Russell, eight. Nate Thurmond of the San Francisco Warriors once had 42; Jerry Lucas of the Cincinnati Royals once had 40.

For nearly two decades, no NBA player has grabbed as many as 40 rebounds in a game, primarily because many teams have two or three virtual 7-foot players on their roster now. In the era when Chamberlain and Russell were grabbing so many rebounds, those two often were up there all by themselves.

Moses Malone's Workouts

Moses Malone led the NBA in rebounds for six consecutive seasons while earning three Most Valuable Player Awards, two with the Houston Rockets and one with the 76ers when they won the 1983 championship. From the time Malone was growing up in Petersburg, Virginia, as the nation's most coveted high school basketball player, he worked harder at improving his rebounding skills than perhaps any other player. At a summer basketball camp once, Dick Vitale, later the Pistons' coach, noticed that Malone had stayed on the court while the other players went to lunch. The teenager was throwing a ball up against the backboard, then jumping and grabbing it, as if it had been a rebound. Time after time, Malone did that until Vitale wandered over.

"Why are you working out all by yourself?" Vitale asked.

"Coach, you got to get the ball before you can shoot it."

At 6-10 and 265 pounds, Malone learned to get the ball and shoot it as nobody else has. Most rebounders are more effective on the defensive backboard, but Malone is considered to be the best offensive rebounder in basketball history.

"When you get an offensive rebound," he has said, "you're right there to shoot it back up."

Before being traded to the Washington Bullets following the 1986 playoffs, Malone was averaging 23.9 points a game over ten NBA seasons. Earlier he had played two seasons in the American Basketball Association, having joined the Utah Jazz out of high school. As a rookie with the Jazz, he averaged 18.8 points and 14.5 rebounds even though he didn't turn twenty years old until late that season. All those rebound drills had prepared him for the hard work under the backboards.

"I've seen Mo do things over guys you wouldn't believe," his 76er teammate Bobby Jones once said. "And he does them when he's dead tired."

As a Houston resident, Malone impressed his work ethic on Hakeem Olajuwon, whom the Rockets chose from the University of Houston as the first selection in the 1984 draft. Olajuwon met Malone at the Fonde Recreation Center, where they played during the summer months. During the 1986 playoffs, Olajuwon was the primary reason why the Rockets needed only five games to eliminate the Lakers, then the defending NBA champions, in the Western Conference final. When that series ended, Magic Johnson shook his head.

"In terms of raw athletic ability," Johnson said, "Hakeem is the best I've ever seen."

Olajuwon averaged more than 11 rebounds a game that season while also averaging 23.5 points.

"Hakeem's cat-quick," Johnson added. "You can't box him out, and he runs the floor."

On the Rockets' roster, Olajuwon was listed at 7 feet and a muscular 250 pounds, but he insisted that he's not quite that tall. Not that it made much difference to any of the other NBA centers, even Kareem Abdul-Jabbar.

"Hakeem plays like a seven-footer," the Laker center said, "so it doesn't matter how he's listed."

Pat Riley, the Laker coach, realized that Olajuwon would be a problem for the Lakers in the Western Conference for years to come, especially after Abdul-Jabbar retired. Unlike many NBA centers, Olajuwon knew only one speed—all-out.

"Centers in this league are supposed to pace themselves," Riley said. "But nobody's told him that, nobody's distorted his mind."

Olajuwon is that rare combination, a strong 7-footer who can jump high. And he uses both attributes to snatch rebounds. But many of the best rebounders are not exceptional leapers. Larry Bird was considered the Celtics' best rebounder, but he did it with fundamentals, not jumping ability.

"In the NBA," Bird said, "a great many players are not sound rebounders, because they don't know the fundamentals. On rebounds I just watch the ball when someone on the opposing team shoots. If I think the shot is going to be short, I move to where I think the ball will come down off the rim, and most of the time I'm right.

"Many players do only one thing at a time when they're rebounding. They'll come down to the basket and box out one time, but the next time they'll come down and just try to follow the ball. You've got to learn to put it all together—to box out and follow the ball. And you've got to learn to put it all together in quick motion."

Kevin McHale and Charles Barkley

Another Celtic forward, Kevin McHale, wasn't a tremendous leaper, but he got rebounds the same way many others do, with a work ethic developed in his Minnesota boyhood.

"My father once cut the tip of his thumb off with a chain saw," McHale once said. "But all he said was 'That hurts.' That was it. My father worked forty-two years in the iron mines and never complained. He never missed a day of work. And people ask me if I'll be able to play basketball on a bad foot."

Kurt Rambis, the Lakers' bespectacled forward, was another non-leaper who worked to position himself under the backboards.

"For me," Rambis said, "there's not much technique involved.

Kevin McHale reaches high.

Sure, everybody gives the other guy a little push here, a little pull there, but jumping high really doesn't mean that much. It's like Bill Russell once said, most of the rebounds are taken below the rim. So what it comes down to is positioning and will."

Where there's a will, there's a way. And for sheer will, Charles Barkley usually gets his way, as his teammates can attest.

"Charles gets us awake," Maurice Cheeks said when they were 76er teammates. "We sometimes get on too low a flame, but then Charles comes along and tears down the backboard, and we remember what we're out there for. We'd better. We don't want Charles to be mad at us."

Barkley is only 6-6, but he's a burly 263 pounds, down from 300 during his college career at Auburn, where he was known as "the Round Mound of Rebound."

"You'd never know Charles was an anemic baby when he was born," his mother, Charcey, said. "His first six months, he had to have blood transfusions, and he was so weak, the transfusions had to be done through his feet. But once we got him home, he just loved to eat and eat. And look at him now."

For all his strength, Barkley is not a great leaper, and his hands are

Although not as tall as others, Charles Barkley (with ball) often plays better.

too small for him to palm a basketball. Although he's listed at 6-6, Barkley contends that he's really only 6-5, shorter than some NBA guards. But he considers that to be a positive influence on his career.

"If I was two or three inches taller," he said, "I probably wouldn't work as hard. I wouldn't have the determination that I have. When I go out there, I go out thinking I'm the best player on the floor. I think I can do anything."

Like every good rebounder, he usually can.

COACHING

"Auerbach, That's Who"

Red Auerbach helped build the Celtics' championship heritage.

SYMBOLS OF THE CELTICS' GLORY, BIG GREEN-AND-WHITE banners hang from the Boston Garden rafters—one for each of their NBA championships. Those banners are a tribute to the players on each of those title teams, notably Bill Russell and Bob Cousy, John Havlicek and Dave Cowens, Larry Bird and Dennis Johnson. But all those banners are also a tribute to the coaches—Red Auerbach during the long reign from 1957 through 1966, Bill Russell in 1968 and 1969, Tom Heinsohn in 1974 and 1976, Bill Fitch in 1981, and K. C. Jones in 1984 and 1986. No other team has won so many NBA championships. No other team has had so many championship coaches.

In basketball, as in any other sport, the value of a coach is sometimes forgotten. No coach has ever won an NBA championship without good players. But not every coach with good players has won a championship.

Of those Celtic coaches who

followed Auerbach, only Fitch had not been a Celtic player. Russell, Heinsohn, and K. C. Jones represent Auerbach's legacy as a coach. Auerbach had the NBA's best players in those years. But would they have been the best if Auerbach had not been their coach?

No, says Bobby Knight, the University of Indiana coach.

"Nobody knew what Russell was going to do until he got to Boston," says Knight, a longtime admirer of Auerbach's coaching philosophy. "Who drafted Sam Jones? Who took people like Satch Sanders and Jim Loscutoff and made them great players? Who took a nonshooting guard like K. C. Jones and made him a superstar? Auerbach, that's who. If any other coach in the NBA drafted someone as quick and agile as Russell, he'd immediately make him into an offensive player. By having Russell concentrate on defense, Auerbach knew exactly what he was doing."

Russell agrees, distinguishing between his performance and the *results* of his performance—all those Celtic championships.

"I would have been the same player," Russell has said. "I never thought there was a better basketball player than me. But would the results have been the same without Red as our coach? I have serious doubts. He was lucky to have me, but I was lucky to have him. I think his presence was necessary. I really do."

Along with all those NBA championships, Red Auerbach developed a Celtic pride and tradition that endured during their few bad seasons, notably a 29-53 record during the 1978–79 season after a 32-50 record the season before.

"I've preached loyalty to every Celtic player who's worn our uniform since 1950," Auerbach once said. "We're a family, I tell them. We care for one another. We're proud of one another. We can always count on one another."

Russell, Heinsohn, and Jones could never be described as clones of Auerbach, who ruled the Celtics' front office for more than twenty years after he stopped coaching. On the bench as well as on display anywhere else, Auerbach often was abrasive and noisy, but he under-

As a coach and player, K. C. Jones was with fifteen title teams.

stood that his Celtic coaches had to be themselves, not try to be like him. Russell had a unique role in that he remained the Celtics' center for three seasons after he was named coach. Russell's personality remained the same—cool on the outside, simmering with competitive heat on the inside. Heinsohn had been a shooter as a 6-6 forward, but as a coach he understood the team concept. K. C. Jones had been a defensive specialist who quickly adapted to the coach's role of teacher.

"You're dealing with twelve different individuals, twelve different personalities," Jones said. "Some guys might be sensitive; others have big egos. The big thing is to get them to play and mesh together and be happy doing it. If you start hammering away at them, you might interfere with their creativity."

Pat Riley's Environment

Pat Riley, who guided the Lakers to the 1982, 1985, 1987, and 1988 championship titles, has described coaching with almost the same words, saying, "All I care about is creating an environment in which the talent can flourish. That means all twelve of our individuals. I have to know as much as possible about each one, to motivate them, to be able to draw them together, to know how to serve them best. I have a role—to organize, to direct, to put you, the player, in position to

win. But then you're going to do the winning or losing, not me."
Sometimes a coach's words put his team into position, as Riley's did
before the second game of the 1985 playoff final.

In the opener, the Celtics had embarrassed the Lakers, 148–114. As
the Lakers got on their team bus to go to the Boston Garden for the
second game, Riley began thinking of his father, Lee, the manager of
the Philadelphia Phillies' baseball farm team in Schenectady, New
York, where Pat went to high school.

"The day I got married in 1970," the Lakers' coach said, "my
father was leaving the wedding reception when he stuck his head out
of the car and said, 'Just remember, somewhere, someplace, some-
time, you're going to have to plant your feet and make a stand. And
when that time comes, you do it.' It turned out those were his last
words to me, because he died of a heart attack soon after that. But
sitting on the bus in Boston that day, I heard that voice again. And
that became my pregame talk, that everyone has a father, that everyone has a voice you respond to. And that for us, this was that place
and that time. And now we all
had to make a stand."

That night the Lakers won,
109–102, and went on to take
the NBA title in six games.

"When the coach spoke of
fathers and voices," Michael
Cooper of the Lakers said, "the
score was already 5–0 for us
before the start. That was appro-
priate. It was subtle. It was dramatic. It was true."

Through his nine seasons as
the Laker coach, Riley had a .733
winning percentage, the highest
in history among NBA coaches

**As the coach
of the Lakers,
Pat Riley "took
the good and
made sure it
stayed good."**

who have been on the bench for more than four hundred regular-season games.

"He's been blessed with good talent," Magic Johnson has said, "but he took the good and made sure it *stayed* good."

After leaving the Lakers following the 1990 playoffs, Riley spent a season as an NBC television studio analyst before becoming the New York Knicks' coach.

"There isn't any game like this game," he said, "that makes you feel more alive."

His emphasis on defense and rebounding suddenly turned the Knicks into a contender.

"Our philosophy," he said, "is predicated on advancement of the ball: get it off the boards or get it out of the net and inbound the ball, advance the ball quickly into a threat position. If there's not a scoring opportunity, then your job is to flow precisely and efficiently into the second part of your offense. All of this cannot happen unless you are defensive-minded and rebounding-oriented and can react instantaneously from a defensive mentality to a transition mentality."

But without the great players he had with the Lakers during their championship years, notably Magic Johnson and Kareem Abdul-Jabbar, Riley was unable to lift the Knicks to the NBA title. In the 1994 playoffs they reached the seventh game of the NBA finals, only to lose when the Houston Rockets, led by Hakeem Olajuwon, won their first of two consecutive championships. After the 1995 playoffs Riley resigned from the Knicks and joined the Miami Heat as part owner, president, and coach.

"Internally, we let down," Riley said of the Knicks. "Every player has to decide if his values coincide with ours."

Phil Jackson's Different Style

Apparently not enough Knicks' values coincided with Riley's values. But those Knicks also had the misfortune to draw the Chicago Bulls, with Michael Jordan at his best, in the playoffs during Riley's first three years: in the opening round in 1991 and in the Eastern Conference final in both 1992 and 1993. Each year the Bulls eliminated the Knicks, then went on to win the championship as their coach, Phil Jackson, developed into one of the NBA's best.

"To me," Jordan said, "Phil is probably the best professional coach as far as getting the best out of his players and maintaining a certain harmony among different personalities."

Jackson was different too. Once a 6-8 sixth-man forward on the 1973 Knicks' championship team, he was devoted to defense, but he also related to players differently from other coaches. With his beard and angular shoulders that made him seem to have a coat hanger inside his jacket, he was a New Age philosopher who discussed Zen Buddhism and the sacred beliefs of the Lakota Sioux, a Native American tribe from his native Montana.

Phil Jackson, coach of the Michael Jordan Bulls.

When he and his Knick teammate Bill Bradley ran a basketball clinic at a South Dakota reservation years ago, he was given the name "Swift Eagle."

His office has several Lakota Sioux artifacts: a bear-claw necklace, an owl feather, a wooden arrow with a tobacco pouch tied to it, a painting depicting the story of Chief Crazy Horse, a picture of a white buffalo calf. Lakota totems decorate the Bulls' meeting room, where Jackson has talked to his players like no other coach.

"Turn the lights down," he once told them. "Breathe. Concentrate."

During the 1993 playoffs in New York, instead of practicing one day, he took the Bulls for a ride on the Staten Island ferry. He has been known to say, "There's more to basketball than basketball," meaning the team concept that he preached in winning four NBA titles: three with Michael Jordan at his best in 1991, 1992, and 1993 and a fourth in 1996 with Jordan, Scottie Pippen, and Dennis Rodman.

"Phil knows how to blend personalities," said Steve Kerr, a Bulls' outside shooter. "A lot of teams would not have been able to accept three guys getting all the attention, but we had no problem with that."

Wherever basketball is played—in the NBA, college, high school, or local church leagues—the coach has to be the boss. Otherwise the team concept is lost, and five players are out there without any plan.

Pete Newell's strategy guided California to the 1959 NCAA title.

The Mentor

Pete Newell has often been described as a mentor of basketball coaches, an adviser on strategy not only to coaches in the NBA, but even to some in junior high school. Only three coaches have

had teams that have won the NCAA championship, the National Invitation Tournament title, and the Olympic gold medal—Bobby Knight, Dean Smith, and Newell. Newell's 1959 University of California team won the NCAA, his 1949 University of San Francisco team won the NIT, and his 1960 United States Olympic team won in Rome, Italy. Although he never coached in the NBA, his theories have influenced virtually every NBA coach.

"Pete raised a lot of us," Bill Fitch said. "He was the first coach to use the crosscourt pass, which was something that everybody said you should never do. His effects on the game are so widespread and are still evident."

"Pete Newell, like Clair Bee and Hank Iba, pioneered basketball concepts," Bobby Knight said. "They were innovative. They set things up in such a way that the rest of us could come along and copy what they did."

Year by year, Knight has developed into something of a mentor himself. More than a dozen of his assistant coaches at Indiana and Army have gone on to be college head coaches. Mike Krzyzewski, the Duke coach, was a guard at Army and later an assistant coach when Knight was there.

"There's an intimidation factor working for him," Krzyzewski said. "But he overcomes that by prompting discussion, by drawing you out."

Knight's 1976, 1981, and 1987 Indiana teams won NCAA titles; his 1984 United States Olympic team won the gold medal at Los Angeles. Throughout his career he has been a heated bench coach, occasionally bursting into flames. To protest an official's call, he once threw a chair across the court. At the 1979 Pan-American Games in San Juan, Puerto Rico, he was arrested after an altercation with a policeman over the arrival of a Brazilian women's team in the gym where his United States team was still practicing. At the 1981 Final Four he stuffed a Louisiana State University rooter into a trash basket. Not that he didn't realize later that he had made mistakes.

"I don't agree," Knight once said in a moment of guilt, "with everything I do."

Amid his controversies, Bobby Knight's Indiana teams have won three NCAA titles.

Dean Smith's Record

But just about everybody in basketball agreed with just about everything that Dean Smith, the North Carolina coach, did in breaking Adolph Rupp's college record of 876 victories.

"In the test of time," said television analyst Bill Raftery, "Dean Smith is in a class by himself."

North Carolina's Dean Smith

Class indeed. In the thirty-six seasons that it took for Smith to surpass Rupp's career total—earned over forty-two seasons at Kentucky—more than 95 percent of Smith's Tar Heel players graduated, and the North Carolina basketball program was never on NCAA probation. Michael Jordan, whose last-second shot won the 1982 NCAA title, perhaps best summed up what it meant to play for the Tar Heel coach.

"I love him like a father," Jordan said. "Maybe I would still be a professional basketball player, but I'm not sure how good I'd be or where I would be playing if I had not played for him. I learned a lot more about basketball than running and dunking. I learned how to play defense. I learned the team concept—how to keep all five players involved and help them play up to their potential."

Many of the best coaches are dictators. Their way is usually the only way. If the players don't do it the coach's way, they don't play for long. But each coach is a dictator in a different way. In his years as the Marquette coach, Al McGuire liked to call himself a "master of ceremonies" instead of a coach.

"I create a party on the court and keep it going," McGuire once said. "I have people with me who do a lot of coaching, but I never know what leg to tell a kid to put out first to make a lay-up."

Maybe not, but McGuire's last Marquette team won the 1977 NCAA title in what he had announced would be his farewell season.

No matter how many NCAA titles a coach wins in the years to come, it's unlikely any will approach John Wooden's record at UCLA of ten championships in twelve years, including seven in succession. In his quietly firm manner, Wooden was a dictator just as much as Bobby Knight has been. The best player Wooden ever had, Kareem Abdul-Jabbar understood the Wooden basketball philosophy.

"John Wooden sees basketball as a very simple game," Abdul-Jabbar said, "and it's his unique talent to hone that simplicity toward perfection. His whole idea is to run with the basketball, beat the defense down the court, play good defense yourself, and get the easiest shots you can get. That's it. He also believed in supreme conditioning and unwavering fundamentals, not only knowing which plays to run and how to run them, but being capable of calling up the physical and emotional stamina at the precise time you need it to win."

In the years since Wooden stopped coaching, only Knight has won three NCAA titles; only Dean Smith (North Carolina), Mike Krzyzewski (Duke), and Denny Crum (Louisville) have won two. Crum had been Wooden's chief assistant at UCLA for several seasons.

"Through the years, I've learned to be patient," Crum has said. "Coach Wooden had tremendous patience. When he said, 'Goodness gracious, sakes alive,' he was swearing at you. He was at the end of the line with you as a player. And as an assistant coach, I had my conflicts with him on the bench as to what to do and who to put in the game. But that was good instead of bad. There's no value in having a 'yes-man' as an assistant coach. You need opinion from your assistants."

But in the NBA or in college or anywhere else, the head coach's opinion is the opinion that counts.

WHY IS BASKETBALL SO POPULAR?

*I*N THE CENTURY SINCE DR. JAMES NAISMITH PUT UP THE peach baskets in the gymnasium in Springfield, Massachusetts, basketball has evolved into one of the world's most popular sports.

Baseball and football have traveled from America to a few other nations, but not many. Basketball, in contrast, has emerged not only as an Olympic sport, but also as a game that is played virtually everywhere throughout the world. One reason is its simplicity. All you need is a ball and a hoop. Another reason is its appeal as a sport that can be played informally with five members on a team. Or four. Or three. Or two. Or even one. In many playgrounds, one-on-one is the basic game. And if there's no one else around, you can play basketball by yourself, a solitary shooter out there aiming a ball at a hoop.

Unlike baseball and football, basketball has another vital appeal: Women and girls can play it in organized youth leagues, in high

The Basketball Hall of Fame in Springfield, Massachusetts

school and college, and on up through the new Women's NBA.

Olympic boycotts in 1980 and 1984 prevented the United States women's team from opposing the Soviet Union team, generally considered the world's best. But in 1986 the Americans twice defeated the Russians in Moscow, winning the Goodwill Games championship and the World Tournament. Cheryl Miller, a 6-3 shooter who had been voted the Outstanding Player Award at the NCAA Women's Final Four in both 1982 and 1983 while at the University of Southern California, led the U.S. team to its 83–60 and 108–88 triumphs.

"Women play a different kind of basketball than men do," said Anne Donovan, the center on those U.S. teams. "Men play above the rim. Women play below the rim."

Donovan and Cheryl Miller, each a member of the 1984 U.S. Olympic gold medal team, were among the first women inducted into the Basketball Hall of Fame, along with Nancy Lieberman-Cline, the first woman to play in a men's professional league. Known as Lady Magic, she was with the 1986 Springfield Fame of the U.S. Basketball League.

"Growing up in New York," Lieberman-Cline has said, "the men's game was a style that I knew, being physical and aggressive."

She knew the men's game because on weekends she would take the subway from Queens to Harlem to play against men in summer leagues. But in assessing the overall women's game, she understood that not every woman could survive in the men's game.

"This is why we work on fundamental skills: dribbling, passing patterns," she said. "Our game is execution because we're not going to overwhelm anybody with physicality."

To some basketball purists, that execution of fundamentals was more appealing than the slam dunk of men's basketball. So was the skill of Sherryl Swoopes, the Texas Tech All-America who was the first woman to have a sneaker named for her, and Rebecca Lobo, the star of the University of Connecticut's undefeated 1995 NCAA champions.

"Ever since I was a little kid who got a poster of the Olympic team at a basketball camp," Lobo said, "I've had it hanging in my room. I saw that poster every day. I never saw women playing professionally on television, so the Olympics was the pinnacle to me."

After helping the U.S. women's team to its 1996 Olympic gold medal in Atlanta, Swoopes and Lobo joined the Women's National Basketball Association that opened in 1997 following the Women's American Basketball League's first season.

Women's basketball in America began to thrive in 1971 when Immaculata, a suburban Philadelphia college, won the first formal national championship. Coached by Cathy Rush, the Mighty Macs also won the next two years. Three members of those teams later emerged as outstanding coaches—Marianne Crawford Stanley at Old Dominion, Rene Muth Portland at Penn State, and Theresa Shank Grentz at Rutgers.

Lisa Leslie was often head and shoulders above opponents in the 1996 Olympic Games in Atlanta.

Lucy Harris, the first dominant center in women's college basketball, led Delta State of Cleveland, Mississippi, to consecutive titles in 1975, 1976, and 1977 before Carol Blazejowski of Montclair State established two scoring records—a 38.6 average as a senior and a 31.7 average over four seasons.

Another reason for basketball's popularity is that, unlike baseball and football, it can be played indoors or outdoors. Most organized games are played in arenas or gymnasiums, but the roots of basketball grow in playgrounds and schoolyards, in driveways and backyards.

Equipment is also relatively inexpensive. Put up a hoop, buy a ball, and put on your sneakers. That's all you need.

But as basketball players grow taller and taller each year, the court seems to have shrunk. For four decades, the standard NBA court has been ninety-four feet by fifty feet. And ever since that railing in Springfield, Massachusetts, happened to be ten feet above the floor, the basket has been ten feet above the floor. The size of the court and the height of the basket remain ideal for college and high school competition. But with the average NBA player taller than 6-7 now, the court is clogged, and virtually every player can slam-dunk the ball.

Some basketball people propose that the court should be larger to provide more room for bigger players, or that only four players should be on a team. But the most popular theory is that the basket should be raised to twelve feet. The traditionalists, however, always mention that no matter how high the basket is, the 7-footers will always be closer to it than the 6-footers.

Debate, of course, is proof of basketball's popularity. If nobody cared about basketball, nobody would bother proposing that the game be changed. In their love for the game, some basketball people are searching for better competition, while others argue that nobody should tinker with what has been a successful game. Go anywhere in the world and youngsters are shooting a ball at a basket, together or alone.

Dr. Naismith would be proud of the game he created—a game that honors him all over the world.

Michael Jordan drives toward the Bulls' 1996 title.

assist   a pass that results directly in a basket

backcourt   the guards who bring the ball up the court and set up their teammates for shots

bounce pass   a pass thrown from one teammate to another, usually on one bounce

box out   to turn your body toward the basket and raise your arms, thereby establishing your position under the backboard and preventing an opposing player from intruding on it

center   usually the team's tallest player, who patrols the area near the basket, both on offense and defense

charging   a personal foul, committed when a player with the ball charges into an opponent who has established defensive position

cross-court pass   a pass thrown from one side of the court to the other side, usually in the offensive zone

double-team   to use two defensive players to cover one offensive player

dunk   to slam or drop the ball into the basket from above the rim

fadeaway   a jump shot during which a player falls backward, away from the basket, in order to avoid having the shot blocked

fast break   to run downcourt quickly, before the opposing team has an opportunity to organize its defense

finger-roll   a shot taken with your hand near the rim, letting the ball roll off your fingers into the basket

foul   illegal contact, by either a defensive player or an offensive player

foul shot or **free throw**   an unhindered shot, worth one point, from the foul line or free-throw line by a player who has been fouled

fullcourt press   a defensive tactic in which each player covers an opposing player closely all over the court, even before the opposing team has put the ball into play

goaltending   interfering with a shot on its downward arc toward the basket, or interfering with a ball that is rolling on the rim of the basket

hook shot or **sky hook**   a high-arcing shot taken, usually by a center, using a sweeping motion with the player's back to the basket after pivoting on the foot opposite to the shooting hand

jump shot   a shot taken after a player has jumped straight up in the air

lay-up or **lay-in**   a shot, usually banked off the backboard, taken from the side of the basket or from in front of the basket

lane or **foul lane**   the area inside the two parallel lines that extend from the foul line or free-throw line to the baseline at each end of the court

man-to-man defense   when each defensive player is assigned a specific offensive player to cover, no matter where that player goes

one-hander   a shot taken with either the right or left hand, usually while jumping in the air but sometimes with both feet on the court

open man   a player without the ball who is in a good position to shoot

pivotman or **post**   a player positioned near the basket who takes a pass, then either pivots to either side while taking a hook shot or throws the ball back to a teammate

point guard or **playmaker**   a backcourt player who brings the ball upcourt, then controls the offense by starting a set play or by throwing a pass to the open man

power forward   a frontcourt player, usually the team's best rebounder

rebound   to grab the ball off either the offensive backboard or the defensive backboard

screen   a play set when an offensive player establishes position in front of a defensive player, thereby enabling a teammate to get free for a shot or a drive to the basket

set shot or **two-hand set**   a two-handed shot, taken from the chest and with both feet on the ground, seldom used now

shooting guard   a backcourt player whose primary role is to shoot rather than to set up plays

small forward   a frontcourt player who is usually a better shooter and a more agile athlete than the power forward

steal   to take the ball away from an offensive player without committing a foul

zone defense   when the defensive players are assigned a specific area (or zone) of the court to cover, rather than being assigned to a particular offensive player